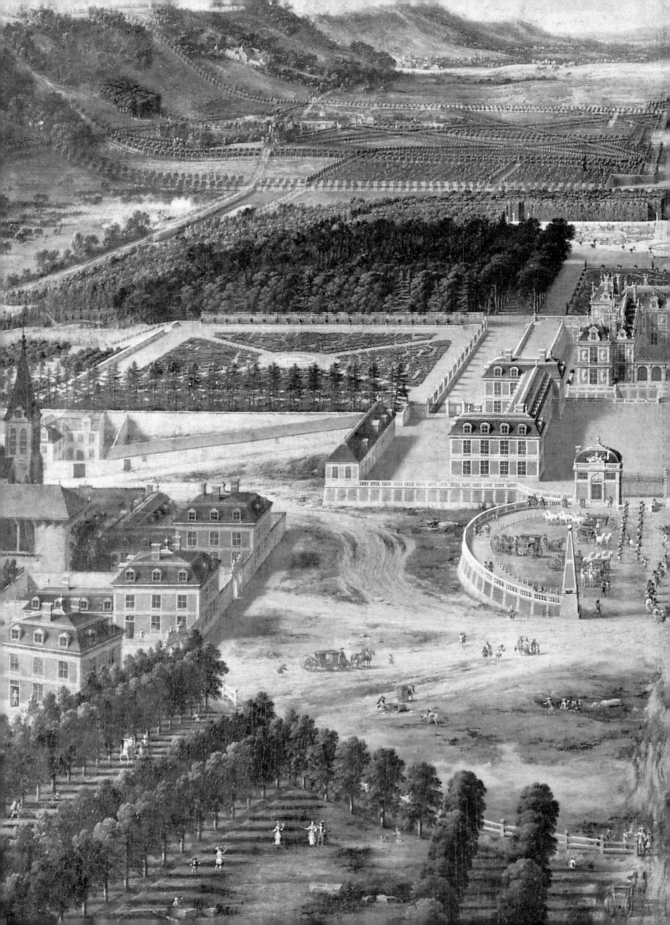

GUY WALTON

LOUIS XIV'S
VERSAILLES

THE
UNIVERSITY OF CHICAGO
PRESS

Guy Walton is associate professor of art history at New York University.

The University of Chicago Press, Chicago 60637
Penguin Books Ltd, Harmondsworth, Middlesex, England

© 1986 Guy Walton

LIBRARY OF CONGRESS CATALOGING-IN-PUBLICATION DATA

Walton, Guy.
Louis XIV's Versailles.

Bibliography: p.
1. Château de Versailles (Versailles, France)
2. Louis XIV, King of France, 1638-1715—Art patronage.
3. France—Social life and customs—17th-18th centuries.
4. France—History—Louis XIV, 1643-1715. I. Title.
NA7736.V5W35   1986   725′.17′0944366   85-8680

I S B N 0-226-87254-8

Contents

PREFACE

There is little need to justify a book on Versailles. The palace in its magnificent garden setting is not only one of the most famous buildings of Western Europe and the most visited national monument of France; it is also one of those places which have passed beyond historical interest and become a part of legend – possibly the most recent building to do so. The kings who built it and lived there, Louis XIII, XIV, XV, XVI, have likewise assumed a special place in history. Not only have their achievements, failures and personalities received the usual historical analyses, but their private lives, and most particularly their life-styles (down to the furniture they sat on, what they ate and their table manners), have proved so interesting that one may speak of a cult of these Bourbons. For many they represent the epitome of civilized living on a very grand scale. Versailles remains to give some idea of that manner of life.

Much of the popular literature on Versailles has stressed the legendary side of its story. People are riveted by the descriptions of a palace whose main apartments were furnished with solid silver furniture and many of the great art works now in the Louvre. Tales – true stories at that – of how the colour scheme and scent of the garden outside the king's bedroom at the Grand Trianon could be changed from morning to evening by the moving of ten thousand flowerpots set into the ground still impress us. Such anecdotes are of course an essential part of any account of the history of Versailles. These were the facts which astounded contemporary visitors and helped to create its unique status. Yet this book has different aims, and will instead present the story of how Versailles came to be a legendary place.

My book proceeds from a very recent view of Louis XIV (1638–1715) and the achievements of his reign. Since 1911 and the publication by Ernest Lavisse of the three volumes of the *Histoire de France* which dealt with Louis's reign, the tendency had been to treat him as a great, even the greatest, king of France, but simultaneously to censure him for his efforts to fulfil the 'ideology of grandeur' which led to such disasters as his long late wars, the economic decline of the late seventeenth century and the revocation of the Edict of Nantes. In more recent scholarly literature, and particularly in the long biography by John Wolf, an alternative approach has emerged. Stress has been laid on the masterful way in which the monarch dealt with most aspects of his government, especially when the intellectual climate and the problems of the era are taken into consideration. An attempt has been made to see Louis in his historical context and to evaluate his achievements in terms of what might be expected of a monarch of the time. The organizational achievements of Louis and his ministers emerge as truly awesome, perhaps the most important aspect of Louis's genius in his 'métier du roy' (the profession of kingship).

One is able to document the history of Versailles as well as any other undertaking of the reign. While it is less glamorous to talk of ground plans and elevations, foundations and walls, than to describe the opulent way of life of Louis's court, it is perhaps more interesting to speak of creativity rather than elegance. We shall observe how specific problems were solved with such brilliance that the public was left with the impression that the achievements of the reign were easily managed and could only have been possible during a very special era, one which Voltaire later claimed was the greatest of the Golden Ages of Western history.

Most serious histories of Versailles have been exhaustive works in several volumes intended to be quasi-complete presentations of the surviving documentation, primarily for reference use. This history attempts to be authoritative but should be readable in a few sittings. It should give the non-specialist an overview of the principal phases of the history of Versailles; it will also go beyond a simple enumeration of the sequence of buildings, gardens and other art works, to provide an account of the reasons for the planning, from the early days of the making of a terraced palace until the completion of the chapel, well into the eighteenth century – more than fifty years of constant activity.

In order to achieve such brevity, much must be omitted. For example, the decision to end the book in 1715 with the death of Louis XIV is somewhat arbitrary. Certainly it may be argued that the contributions of the reigns of Louis XV and XVI, particularly to the interiors and the gardens, represented no decline in quality, and in certain instances may even be of a higher aesthetic merit. On the other hand the present format sets forth clearly the unique achievement of one of the greatest patrons in the history of Western art.

Even dealing only with the era of Louis XIV it was necessary to be highly selective, which has some unfortunate results. Versailles is part of the history of architecture, of gardens, of painting, of sculpture and, not least, of the decorative arts. Ideally, a history should present a capsule view of each of these areas, so that, for example, a reader dipping here and there would be able to follow the history of French sculpture as it relates to Versailles. Yet such an aim would have excessively lengthened the book, and so the history of each of the arts, with the possible exception of the architecture, is only partly covered. This is particularly true of the discussion of the fascinating subject of furniture, which has been treated only at the very few points where documented pieces or evidence of their appearance has survived; and no account whatever of the Louis XIV style has been attempted. Occasionally the selection of the aspects of the art of Versailles covered in each of the periods has proved rather arbitrary, though wherever possible the topics chosen reflect the character of the principal projects of the period in question.

A very few notes on the text are provided at the end of the book to indicate the sources of some quotations and to record instances where my debt to another writer seemed to require specific acknowledgement. These notes and the reading suggestions at the end of the book will provide, it is hoped, introductions to the basic scholarly studies of various aspects of Versailles and to the locations of fundamental scholarly materials, such as the holdings of original or early drawings and views. The written documents, such as payments, including both printed ones and the partially published holdings of the archives, are described for those wishing to pursue in greater detail some of the many aspects of this complex subject.

ACKNOWLEDGEMENTS

This book has been under way since the autumn of 1972, when a sabbatical leave from New York University allowed me to spend a year in France and to make a study trip to Sweden to do the basic research. Since it was my goal to see Versailles from top to bottom and to study as many as possible of the surviving original drawings and plans, both published and unpublished, and also to look at all the early views (prints and paintings), I have tried the patience of a large number of librarians, curators and archivists. First and foremost at the Musée du Château at Versailles, Pierre Lemoine, Simone Hoog, Daniel Meyer, and Christian Baulez were unfailingly generous and helpful, not only with their time but with information and ideas. Many of their ideas have in time fused with mine, to the extent that I may not always have given them the credit they deserve in the text and notes.

In Paris I was similarly welcomed at the Cabinet des Estampes of the Bibliothèque Nationale, the Archives Nationales and the Institut d'Art et d'Archéologie, to whose staffs I am deeply indebted for their patience and help.

At the library of the Institut de France, I was allowed to study at leisure and to photograph an album of drawings from the collection of Robert de Cotte, and the librarian, Madame Hautecœur, very kindly had one sheet (Fig. 44) 'lifted' for me, to reveal a gallery. I found the same generosity at the library of the École des Beaux Arts, whose librarian, Madame Bouchot-Rabot, allowed me to publish an important elevation of the terrace (Fig. 42); and at the Cabinet des Dessins of the Louvre, Rosaline Bacou, Geneviève Monnier and their colleagues were most helpful and pleasant.

I cannot adequately acknowledge the help of a number of colleagues and friends in France. They gave me both information and intellectual stimulation: to Yves Bottineau, François Souchal and Jacques Thuillier my book owes a substantial debt.

In Stockholm, the drawings department of the Nationalmuseum was no less hospitable, and I remember gratefully Ulf Johnsson, then curator of the architectural holdings, and the Countess von Rosen.

As I began to order my thoughts on this vast subject I was particularly grateful to Peter and Laurie Fusco of Los Angeles, to Gillian Wilson of Malibu and to E. J. Johnson and Whitney Stoddard of Williamstown, who arranged for the University of Southern California, the Los Angeles County Museum, the J. Paul Getty Museum and Williams College to sponsor two series of lectures. These formed a first draft of the present text.

Most of the book was written at New York University overlooking Washington Square; this was made possible by the generous cooperation of the Library of the Institute of Fine Arts at N.Y.U. and the University's Elmer Holmes Bobst Library. They exceptionally allowed me to keep important books in my office for unusually long periods of time.

A number of experts on Versailles have stimulated me by their company and conversation on various occasions as well as by their important writings. Among these are Gerold Weber, Jörg Garms, Margaret Stuffman, Richard Swain, Thomas Hedin, Howard Adams and Betsy Rosasco.

The completion of my research would not have been possible without the financial assistance of the New York University Arts and Science Research Fund, which paid in part for two trips to France for archive work. Two half-year sabbatical leaves in 1976 and in 1980 provided the time for the writing of much of this book. My friend Roger Poirier also gave me a small subsidy in the form of the loan on various occasions of his flat in Montrouge.

Joan Levenstein typed nearly the entire first draft from my handwritten manuscript with the exception of some pages done by Norma Santurri. Joan Kinzer both edited and retyped most of the final version, which was completed by M. J. Vogelsang. Susan Rose-Smith laboured long and hard over the photo orders to fill important *lacunae* in my collection.

Hugh Honour and John Fleming are the godfathers of this book, since it was written at their request, and from the outset they have made valuable suggestions. Peter Carson asked many probing questions and helped with the rewriting of several parts of the text.

My wife Carola has provided constant encouragement and has suffered both the joys and the inconvenience of a number of necessary sojourns abroad. My son Hugh saw the light of day first at Neuilly-sur-Seine because I was in Paris at work on this project. Since it is Carola and Hugh whose lives have been most greatly affected by this work, it is they who have my deepest gratitude.

New York
March 1983

THE PERSIAN EMBASSY
EXTRAORDINARY
(19 FEBRUARY TO 13 AUGUST 1715)

It was alleged by the Duke de Saint-Simon in his famous memoirs that the Persian embassy was something of a fake. He called the ambassador 'highly dubious' and saw the whole business as something arranged by Pontchartrain, the foreign minister, to flatter the old king. There was no pressing reason for an alliance with Persia, and the embassy was regarded by those involved as important primarily because it recalled the good old days of the 1680s and especially the brilliant embassy from Siam (1686).

The last public appearance of Louis XIV's life was the farewell visit of Mohammed Riza Bey (Fig. 1) on 13 August 1715. Although the ceremony was truncated, moved at the last minute from the grand setting of the Hall of Mirrors, where the initial interview had taken place, to the throne room, Louis, who had only recently fallen ill, was able to stand through the long farewell speeches and thus bring to a fitting end the last public showing of his achievements as builder and patron of the arts.

Louis XIV died at a time when a long period of war had come to an end and his country was distinctly on the mend. Things were going well enough to pretend that the greatest days of the reign were not just a distant memory but might be susceptible to partial revival. The accumulated artistic riches and the great buildings of his reign required only maintenance rather than important capital expenditures to provide a sumptuous background for the life of the court.

The Persian ambassador was uniquely privileged to view much of Louis's Versailles with the king still present and living in the style he had so carefully refined, surrounded by a vast court. A description of the ambassador's visit should provide a good introduction to the huge royal residence, almost a city in itself, at the brief period when Louis's works were complete and it was still in use.

Mohammed Riza Bey was housed in Paris at the Hôtel des Ambassades Extraordinaires. His experience of Louis XIV's grandeur began on 19 February 1715, as he travelled the seventeen-mile road to Versailles to his

1. *Antoine Watteau:* The Persian Ambassador, Mohommed Risa Bey. *Drawing, red and black chalk on paper. Inscribed: 'Portrait de l'ambassadeur de Perse Mehemet Riza Bey/Intendant de la province d'Erivan./qui fit son entré a paris le 7 février 1715/Dessiné d'après nature par Antoine Vateau, il est gravé dans l'œuvre de ce maître'*

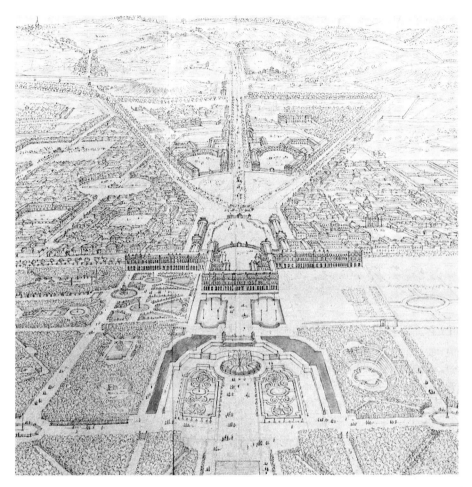

2. Israel Silvestre: bird's-eye
view from the west of the
avenues, château, town and
gardens of Versailles.
Drawing, c. 1684

reception. Most of the route was through forests of the royal hunting
preserves, such as the Bois de Boulogne and the forest of Saint Cloud, which
alternated with more open farmland. He crossed the river Seine, and arrived
at Versailles by the enormously wide Avenue de Paris.

The approach to Versailles from Paris, the route taken by most visitors,
was from the east and the last part had been laid out shortly after Louis
assumed personal rule in 1661. Three wide roads lined with large trees
approached the château in a 'patte d'oie' or goose foot, and converged in
front of the main entrance (Fig. 2). The approach was managed so as to
afford fine views of the château from the two main roads to it as they passed
over the crest of a small hill, views celebrated more than once by the royal
topographical painters (Fig. 3). The hill was high enough to serve as the
location of one of the several reservoirs which fed the fountains of the park.

From the Avenue de Paris the ambassador must hardly have been aware that a town existed in the vicinity of the château, since it had been cleverly relegated to areas north and south of the approach roads in order to preserve something of the country atmosphere of the place. But by 1715 Versailles was almost a city.

The area between the three avenues, that which would have been seen on the official approach, was kept as green as possible. Some hôtels and pavilions were to be found there, separated from one another by areas of grass and trees. One hôtel was the royal kennels, another the residence of one of Louis's natural daughters.

The main part of the town, to the north, was the most densely built up and contained a parish church, two large squares and another which served as an open-air market. There was also a large complex of buildings, once the royal stables, which had been given to the queen and on her death to Louis's heirs.

The southern area was perhaps wrongly characterized as town at all. Although this had been the old village of Versailles, Louis had destroyed the parish church and commandeered much of the area for his own use. Near the château stood the huge Grand Commun, where many of his staff were fed and housed. Another large space was taken up by the Potager du Roi, the world-famous fruit and vegetable garden presided over by the great La Quintinie until his death in 1688. But there was also room for the superintendency of royal buildings, several ministries and two convents, of which the Recollets was the most important.

At the convergence of the three avenues at the entry to a large square, the space between them was occupied by the mammoth 'great' and 'little' stables of the king, which could house about 12,000 horses (Fig. 4). The château itself was opposite these, atop a rather large hill and dominating the town. Indeed, Hardouin-Mansart had been forced to build a squat parish church because no building in Versailles could be higher than Louis's château.

The gilded metal grille (see Fig. 4) which provided the principal entry to the château complex was on the far side of a vast open space at the precise point of the convergence of the three avenues. The grille was also located low enough on the hill so as not to obscure any important part of the buildings when viewed from the avenues. On either side of the main entry gate were piers topped with statues of allegorical figures, which marked the start of the vast system of terracing leading gently up the hill to the royal residence.

Beyond the grille a distant central façade of red brick and stone, crowned with sculptured decoration, dominated a sequence of wings which reached out towards the visitor (see Fig. 4). Only on close inspection could it be

3 (opposite). J.B. Martin: view from the heights to the east of Versailles (M.V. 749). Painting

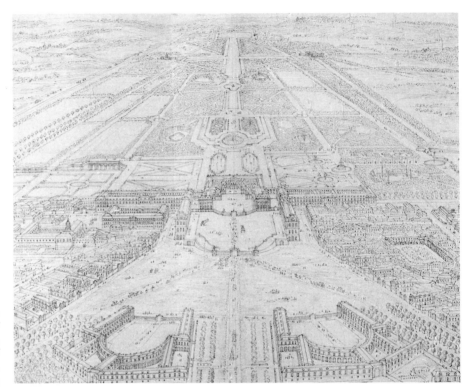

4. Israel Silvestre: bird's-eye view from the east of the stables, Place d'Armes, château and gardens of Versailles (Inv. 34216). Drawing, c. 1684

seen that the buildings nearest the front grille were detached from the château above. They were known as the Wings of the Ministries and in 1715 still served the government rather than the personal needs of the king. They flanked a second large open area known as the Cour d'Armes. At the time of the embassy, numbers of the household troops must have been lined up for the arrival, their varied and colourful uniforms adding an impressive spectacle.

Another pair of forward-reaching wings just behind the Wings of the Ministries ended in twin colonnades. With these the main building began, and another grille stretched across the front of the château between the two colonnades, defining the end of the Cour d'Armes and creating a second courtyard, further east, for the château itself (Fig. 5). Most coaches had to stop before this second grille, and people visiting the château generally proceeded on foot; however, some individuals of high rank who enjoyed the much coveted right of entry to the inner court of the Louvre in Paris were allowed to pass through.

The Marquis of Dangeau recounts that just before the ambassador arrived the king made a brief appearance on the balcony of his chamber.

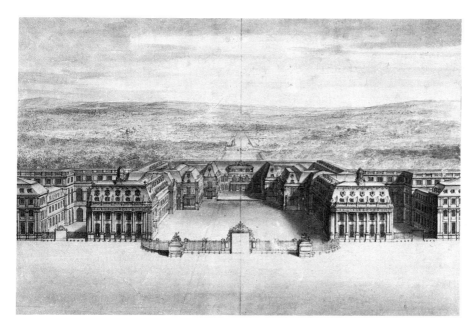

5. Anonymous: view from the east of the central court area of the château of Versailles. Drawing, 1680s

Louis wore a gold and black cloak decorated with diamonds worth twelve and a half million *livres*, and many other jewels, some borrowed from various princes. There was a great crowd. Even the roofs of the château held spectators, and the public apparently burst into acclamations of 'Vive le roi!' on seeing the king, who was delighted by the enthusiasm of the people for this occasion.

Shortly after Louis's appearance, Mohammed Riza Bey, who had already left his coach for a horse, rode up. The upper court where he dismounted was unusual in its shape, for the two side wings did not reach directly out from the central façade but were formed by a sequence of three projections, so that the court widened as it approached the Cour d'Armes. The whole forecourt area is best understood as three connected but separate court-yards, the inmost of which was raised up a few steps and paved not with stones but with black and white marble slabs. These gave it its special name, the Cour de Marbre. The sculptural decoration of the building was profuse, particularly at the level of the roof. The ambassador may have known that the king's bedroom (Fig 6), where he awaited the embassy, was on the floor above in the very centre of the façade, directly below the central gable (see Fig. 32).

The principal entrances to both the château and the gardens were in this forecourt. On the ground floor around this court were apartments which served mainly for the royal guards and for administrative purposes. One

6. The bedroom of Louis XIV at Versailles seen from the east (window) wall side (C.C. 174). Drawing, after 1702

ground-floor room was specially prepared for the reception of important visitors. There the ambassador met some of the officers of the household and waited until the king was ready to receive him.

Shortly after eleven a.m., Mohammed Riza Bey proceeded up the slope of the court almost to the steps leading to the marble paving of the Cour de Marbre. On each side of the court at that level there were triple arches enclosed by gilt grilles. He entered one of those on the north, inside which was a vestibule of coloured marble, and then ascended the grandiose double Stairway of the Ambassadors, also resplendent with coloured marbles and in part painted by Charles Le Brun (Fig. 7).

The principal reception rooms and those where the king lived were one flight up. It is recorded that the ambassador was led through the Grand Apartment of the King, which served as the apartment of state. A contemporary ground plan shows the rooms through which the ambassador moved (Fig. 8). The apartment was arranged *en enfilade*, which means that the rooms were aligned, as were their doorways, so that one could proceed through them from east to west (bottom to top on the plan) in a straight line. It is likely that he was shown the whole apartment. First, the two marble vestibules at the head of the stairs, the Salon of Venus (29 on the plan) and that of Diana (28), so-called from the subjects of their painted ceilings (Fig. 9). Then came the Salon of Mars (27 on the plan), the largest room of the suite, whose long interior south wall contained two musicians'

galleries (supported by columns) flanking a central fireplace. The gilt and painted ceiling here was similar to those of the preceding rooms, but the upper parts of this salon's walls were covered with crimson brocade and hung with some of the greatest paintings of the royal collection, including canvases by Raphael, Lotto, Cortona and Guercino, the famous *Supper at Emmaus* by Veronese and Le Brun's *Alexander and the Family of Darius*, his best-known work.

It is unlikely that Mohammed Riza Bey would have paused to look out at the view (Fig. 10), but from the windows he could have seen the long wall of the north wing of the château, which ran at right angles to the axis of the *enfilade*. (The wing can also be seen in Fig. 2, to the left of the central portion of the château.) This substantial extension of the building, which is larger than t'e central garden façade, would have suggested a palace more vast than it had appeared from the other side, where he had arrived. Still more of the château would have come into view much later, since the north wing represented only slightly more than a third of the total expanse of the garden front of Louis's palace. The ambassador might also have noted that a warm-coloured yellow/white stone had been used for the exterior and that orders of columns and pilasters added an effect both more stern and certainly more grand than the red brick of the entrance side.

Had he inquired, the ambassador would have learned that most of the north wing housed senior courtiers. Some other rooms adjoining the Grand

7. *J.M. Chevotet: the Stairway of the Ambassadors, formerly at Versailles. Engraving*

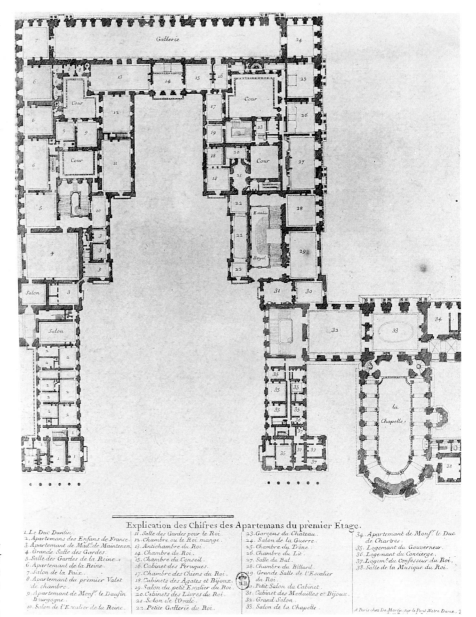

8. *Plan of the Premier Étage and the Apartments of the King and Queen of the royal château of Versailles (the De Mortin plan). Engraving, after 1702*

1. Le Duc Dudin.
2. Apartemans des Enfans de France.
3. Apartemant de Madᵉˡ de Maintenon.
4. Grande Salle des Gardes.
5. Salle des Gardes de la Reine.
6. Apartemant de la Reine.
7. Salon de la Paix.
8. Apartemant du premier Valet de chambre.
9. Apartemant de Monsʳ le Daufin Brurgogne.
10. Salon de l'Escalier de la Reine.
11. Salle des Gardes pour le Roi.
12. Chambre ou le Roi mange.
13. Antichambre du Roi.
14. Chambre du Roi.
15. Chambre du Conseil.
16. Cabinet des Peruques.
17. Chambre des Chiens du Roi.
18. Cabinets des Agates et Bijoux.
19. Salon du petit Escalier du Roi.
20. Cabinets des Livres du Roi.
21. Petite Gallerie du Roi.
22. ...
23. Garçons du Chateau.
24. Salon de la Guerre.
25. Chambre du Trône.
26. Chambre du Lit.
27. Salle du Bal.
28. Chambre du Billard.
29. Grande Salle de l'Escalier du Roi.
30. Petit Salon du Cabinet.
31. Cabinet des Medailles et Bijoux.
32. Grand Salon.
33. Salon de la Chapelle.
34. Apartemant de Monsʳ le Duc de Chartres.
35. Logemant du Gouverneur.
36. Logemant du Concierge.
37. Logemᵗ du Confesseur du Roi.
38. Salle de la Musique du Roi.

A Paris chez De Martin, sur le Pont Notre Dame.

Apartment at the near end of the wing provided for passage from the apartment to the chapel and were decorated as vestibules. At the far end of the building (which was not quite finished behind the façade), room was left for a large theatre or opera house.

The ambassador next crossed the Salon of Mercury (26 on Fig. 8), rather smaller than the room which preceded it. A full third of this room was separated from the rest by a balustrade behind which, on a dais, was a large bed of state, canopied and hung with rich fabrics. Moving on to the next room of the apartment, the Salon of Apollo (25 on Fig. 8), the ambassador may have noted that things were not quite in their normal order. The room was very similar to the Salon of Mercury. It was almost certainly hung with pictures, though Louis did possess some splendid embroideries which were apparently hung on special occasions such as this (see Fig. 21). Normally it served as the throne room and the room contained a dais with a canopy above it, but the dais would have been without the throne because it had been moved for this particular occasion. All of the rooms of the Grand

9. South wall of the Salon of Diana (with Gian Lorenzo Bernini's bust of Louis XIV), Grand Apartment of the King. Versailles

Apartment were lavishly furnished with tables, consoles, stands for the candelabra, upholstered stools and the like, either of gilt wood or with inlays of rare woods and tortoiseshell with applied gilt metal. The most eminent furniture-maker of the time, Boulle, was probably responsible for more than a few of these, since it was traditional for the Salon of Apollo to be decorated with particularly splendid pieces (see Fig. 122). In all likelihood most of the rooms of the apartment would also have contained whatever small trees and flowers the expertise of the king's gardeners could produce in winter. There may well have been bouquets of forced bulbs on the candle-stands (unused in the daylight) as well as the usual orange and jasmine trees standing in urns against the walls and between the windows.

It was the intention of the crown that the visit should be an experience in which the brilliance of the palace was expected to work its effect gradually, but there was also an attempt to increase the brilliance along the route to the point of overwhelming the visitor as he proceeded. The room following the Salon of Apollo was a case in point. Unlike the previous rooms, which were lighted just from their north walls, this room, the Salon of War (24 on Fig. 8), had windows on both north and west sides (see Fig. 66). The decorators had cleverly exploited the increased light, creating a decor which was unlike the stone of the vestibules and the paintings, gilt and textiles of the rest of the apartment. Here the coloured marble was enhanced by reliefs of trophies executed in gilt bronze, the ceiling was decorated with deeply modelled gilt plaster and the light played over the surfaces, with panels of mirror adding to the brilliant effect.

But the Salon of War can hardly have had time to make a lasting impact, since it was a turning-point in the route of the procession (see Fig. 8, No. 24) and in mid-room the greatest wonder of Versailles, the Hall of Mirrors, opened before the ambassador (Fig. 11). The vastness of that space must have made the ample proportions of the Grand Apartment seem insignificant.

While the Hall of Mirrors may not be among the largest vaulted spaces in Western architecture, in its context it is unique in terms of its impact. Seventy-five metres long, ten wide, the gallery alone is just slightly shorter in its length than all of the six rooms the ambassador had just passed through. The vaulted and painted ceiling rose to a height of about one and two-thirds storeys. Lighted in its entire length by seventeen large windows facing west and by the reflections from mirrors on the other side, the gallery was decorated like the previous salon, an opulent interior of glistening marble, sparkling mirrors, shining gilt bronze ornaments, and crowned with Le Brun's decorative masterpiece of a painted ceiling commemorating Louis's victories in the Dutch Wars of the 1670s.

Such a setting, particularly when complete with its furnishings of pedestals supporting antique sculptures and vases, consoles, candelabra stands and urns with small flowering trees, would have been dazzling enough for any occasion. But for this embassy it was further elaborated. The south end of the gallery was spanned by a structure of eight steps to hold the throne. (This dais obscured the Salon of Peace, which formed a symmetrical pendant to the Salon of War and was decorated in a similar manner.) The entire floor of the gallery as well as the steps to the throne were covered with some of the great carpets made for the king at the Savonnerie manufactory. The painting of the event by Antoine Coypel (Fig. 12) also shows large temporary decorations in the shape of figures of Fame mounted upon pedestals along the walls. The courtiers had been commanded to appear in full court dress with their best jewels.

After meeting the king, the ambassador retired downstairs and was served dinner by the Grand Master (Fig. 13). Afterwards, he was shown another important part of the château, the Grand Apartment of the Queen, unused for some time since the death of the dauphine, the Duchess of Burgundy, but now chosen for the formal visit to the child dauphin, her son. The ambassador was probably taken up the Queen's Stairway (Fig. 14), across

11 (opposite). The Hall of Mirrors viewed from the north end

12. Antoine Coypel: the reception of the Persian ambassador in the Hall of Mirrors on 19 February 1715 (M.V. 5641). Painting

13. Anonymous: déjeuner of the Persian ambassador at Versailles. Pencil and ink drawing

14. The Queen's Stairway, Versailles

the court on the south side of the château, opposite the Stairway of the Ambassadors, smaller but richly decorated in marble, bronze and gilt. It is not clear in which room the prince received him: possibly in the salon called the Grand Couvert, where the king had dined with the queen when she was alive. If so, the procession moved from the stairway through the richly marbled vestibule called the Queen's Guards' Room (5 on Fig. 6; see also Fig. 71) and then into the long room behind it (6 on Fig. 6). But the reception may have been in the Queen's Chamber, in which case a further anteroom was crossed on the way. These rooms were intended to be similar to those of the Grand Apartment of the King, and had the same ceilings of gilt plaster inset with paintings of Greek gods and histories. The walls were also covered with brocade hangings and pictures. From these rooms the great south wing could be seen to the right of the garden façade (see Fig. 2). Similar to the north wing, it contained for the most part the apartments of the king's immediate family.

It is not clear whether Mohammed Riza Bey was given a tour of the gardens. If so, it was hardly on the day of the great reception, but more probably in the more clement weather of the summer. It is hard to imagine that no attempt would be made to impress the ambassador with the park, since the gardens were the pride of the king, who even took the trouble to write in his own hand a guide to them for visitors. It is also likely that engravings of some of the most important features of the gardens were included among the gifts offered to the ambassador (see for example Fig. 18).

The park which began at the château and extended far to the south, west and north was divided into two parts, a huge hunting terrain and a vast walled 'little' park (Petit Parc; see Fig. 15). The large hunting park had been developed largely by land improvement, such as the filling of bogs, and by the creation of wide forest paths to allow for the more convenient movement of the hunting parties. The Petit Parc, on the other hand, was one of the greatest and most influential gardens of the West.

Years before Le Nôtre had shaped the Petit Parc from the substantial hill on which the château stood. He left standing a good part of the woods he found there and, gradually and at very great expense, developed the gardens on three axes at right angles to one another, aligned with three major points of the compass and the château. Since the hill was very steep in all three directions the woods were penetrated with grand vistas. In two directions he extended his carefully contrived views further through the forest by means of artificial areas of water, the Grand Canal and the Pool of the Swiss.

The large areas of the Petit Parc which remained wooded were not without decoration. Here and there, hidden from the main *allées*, they opened up

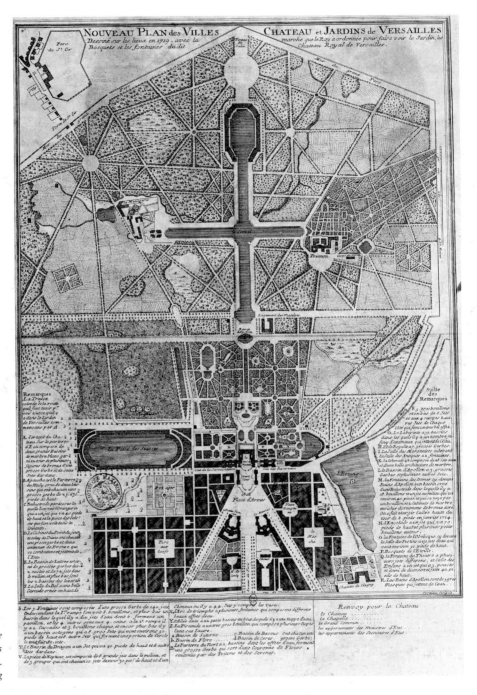

15. New plan of the town, château and gardens of Versailles, 1719. Engraving

16 (opposite). J.B. Martin: bird's-eye view of the north axis of the park of Versailles seen from above the Basin of Neptune (M.V. 751). Painting, c. 1700

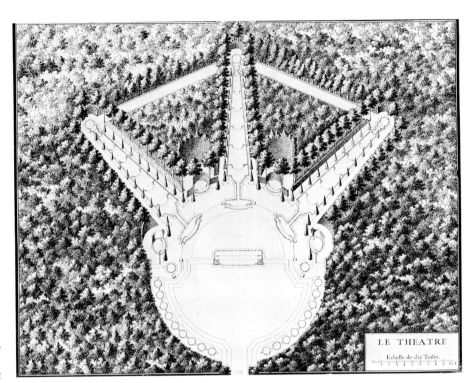

17. Le Théâtre d'eau, *the water theatre* bosquet. *Drawing*

18. Israel Silvestre: view of the Bosquet of the Three Fountains in the garden of Versailles. Engraving, 1684

to form outdoor rooms known as bosquets, which frequently contained fountains, or groupings of several fountains; there were ponds, a ballroom (Fig. 99) and even a famous water theatre (Fig. 17). A large area was occupied by a labyrinth, decorated throughout with relatively small fountains in which painted lead animal figures illustrated the *Fables* of Aesop, an amenity perhaps added years before for the education of Louis's only legitimate son, Monseigneur (Fig. 46).

In the great park and beyond there were four structures which played an important part in the activities at Versailles. The oldest of these was the zoo (Ménagerie), which included buildings with apartments for resting and rooms for dining overlooking the animal enclosures (see Fig. 24). The Ménagerie had been beautifully remodelled about fifteen years earlier for the young dauphin's mother, the Duchess of Burgundy; but it was not much used after her sudden death in 1712. The Grand Canal, which from the château appeared as a straight path of water, was deceptively shaped, since near its far end it was crossed by a north–south branch (see Fig. 15), and the zoo lay off in the woods at the south end of this cross waterway. At the north end of the cross canal was the Grand Trianon (Fig. 110), a lovely one-storey marble and stone building considered a château in its own right.

On the north side of the town of Versailles, rising behind a large pool, was the château of Clagny. It too had gardens of renown, best seen from its galleries and salons. Built in the 1670s for Louis's mistress Madame de Montespan, in 1715 it was in the possession of Louis's favourite among her children by him, the Duke of Maine.

The formal nature of Mohammed Riza Bey's embassy and his religion meant that a few of the principal areas of the château itself were not on his itinerary. Ironically, the most brilliant recent addition to Versailles was among these, the splendid new chapel, made of stone and elaborately decorated on the outside with carved ornament and figure sculpture, which had been consecrated in 1710 and rose well above the level of the roofs of the north wing of the château (Fig. 140).

The living quarters of the king, substantially refurbished since the turn of the century, were probably missed as well, because of the official character of the visit. A visit here of the sort often made by such eminences, who were received in the king's chamber (Fig. 6), would have begun at the Queen's Stairway, then turned away from the Queen's Grand Apartment towards the white and gold rooms along a north–south axis (see Fig. 134). These were located around the Cour de Marbre.

Most visitors to Versailles were particularly dazzled by a set of apartments almost totally forgotten today. These adjoined the king's apartment on the north side of the château and faced for the most part the Cour de

Marbre. Known as the Small (*Petit*) Apartment of the King, these rooms contained some of the more precious treasures of the royal collection and a famous painted ceiling by Mignard (see Fig. 100).

There were yet other apartments worth a visit under this vast roof, but for reasons such as the recent family history of the king they were probably not shown often. On the ground floor in the south-central area of the château, overlooking the gardens, was the apartment of Monseigneur, Louis's former heir, which included a very famous cabinet by Boulle. But Monseigneur had died unexpectedly in 1711, which would have made any formal visit unlikely in a court where no one was allowed to speak of the dead. The great Apartment of the Baths on the ground floor in the north-west corner of the central block of the château must still have retained much of its brilliant decor of coloured marble, reliefs and sculpture even at this late date, and in 1715 it belonged to Louis's favourite son, the Duke of Maine. However, given its age of forty-five years it could hardly have been considered an artistically important area.

At the time of the Persian embassy the creation of impressive buildings and lavish patronage of the arts were seen as unmistakable signs of a great reign. Only military success might be ranked as rather more important. What Mohammed Riza Bey saw, though because of its enormous scale he could hardly have remembered much of the detail, was certainly enough to suggest the truly awesome achievements of a talented monarch who, during the longest reign in the history of France, had had the time, the organizational abilities and the resources to realize a substantial part of his ideal residence. Versailles must have confirmed for the ambassador the idea that he was treating with a truly great king, and if this was indeed the impression he took away with him, he would have shared the view of many of his contemporaries.

THE KING,
HIS ARCHITECTS
AND ADMINISTRATORS

Recently the suggestion has been made that Louis XIV was himself the designer of important buildings at Versailles.[1] His criticisms and suggestions on the many revisions of the plans for the Grand Trianon, particularly during the absence of his sick chief architect, shaped the palace to such an extent that it could possibly be attributed to the king himself. Louis's influence at Versailles went substantially beyond the articulation of his own needs. No detail of interior decoration was too small to interest him. There was a standing order that everything was to be submitted to the king with alternative propositions, and either the king himself or his superintendent then noted the royal decision (often directly on the drawing). But this procedure does not justify an attribution of most of the designs to Louis himself.

Louis XIV was very much a man of his time, deeply impressed by some aspects of Cartesian philosophy (though he prohibited its being taught at the Sorbonne). He firmly believed in the effectiveness of logic, reason and debate, and agreed with many of the advanced minds of his time that truth, or, rather, the best solution to a problem, was most likely to be reached by reasoned debate. Effective planning would come from clear and rational minds – not necessarily from experts in the subjects under discussion. Louis believed that with sufficient intellect, application and time nearly every problem could be solved. These attitudes were reflected in the manner of the planning of Versailles.

Louis's first great superintendent of buildings, the head of the King's Buildings Office (*Bâtiments du Roi*), was Jean-Baptiste Colbert (1619–83), the king's chief adviser on political, economic, naval and religious as well as artistic matters. He was an organizational genius and, at Versailles, the prime mover behind a new approach to architectural planning. He should be considered co-creator with the king of the organization without which Versailles could not have come into being. Colbert encouraged rationality throughout the administration of the kingdom. And he has been quoted apocryphally as saying 'Why use one architect when the best ideas of five responding to the same problems would obviously produce a better solution?' Colbert also kept careful records.

Until 1667 the superintendency of buildings had primarily functioned as a coordinating agency, running competitions, hiring architects and the like. Some time shortly thereafter Colbert decided to transform it into what we today might call an in-house organization. As late as June 1669 various well-known architects were still being asked for plans for the same project for Versailles, so it was probably only after the untimely death of the architect Louis Le Vau (1631?–1670) that the character of the superintendency really took shape. (It should be noted that no successor to Le Vau was appointed for seven years, and yet work never stopped. The explanation for this clearly is that a highly competent staff was able to meet all the needs of the royal household.) Jules Hardouin-Mansart (1646–1708) seems to have fully understood what Colbert had created and to have shaped his career accordingly, emerging during the 1670s as a new type of professional – in name an architect but essentially an administrator-coordinator.

The architectural process became a kind of dialogue between the professionals, who knew the necessary technology and were also experienced judges in questions of aesthetics, and the administrators, who understood such issues as the functional needs of the court and government, the finances available etc. Gradually it seems to have been considered preferable for all parties to work closely at most stages of planning, in a kind of committee approach. This process, well-known in our time, may be considered an important innovation of the administration of Louis XIV.

As time passed, the superintendency and its creative sub-agencies became bastions of privilege. A closed shop emerged, with only those inside able to obtain access to important royal patronage. Colbert, Mansart and the king exploited this situation, combining lucrative and prestigious commissions and positions with more routine assignments, thus producing throughout Versailles work of the highest artistic competence.

The hothouse atmosphere of the King's Buildings Office had in it the potential for greatness, the achievement of an astonishingly high standard of performance, and the possibility of degenerating from petty politics into confusion and inefficiency. In the final analysis it was the will of the king alone which made things work, and he alone surmounted most difficulties. Louis was omnipresent. He could cut right through the complex net of artistic politics and clarify lines of authority. He could flatter and praise or show disfavour, and keep many temperamental artists firmly in line, accepting his authority and, most important of all, working together diligently.

Louis maintained control by serving as godfather to the children of those most in his favour and, more importantly, by providing special pensions which gave some security to those working in professions whose rewards were notoriously uncertain.

The king was much more than the *raison d'être* for Versailles. He took full responsibility for and had veto power over everything. Whether he actually designed any buildings is another question and not a very important one. He himself took credit for only one work at Versailles, the Bosquet of the Three Fountains (Fig. 18), a minor creation.

THE TASTE
OF THE OCCUPANTS

Like many residences Versailles grew in response to the demands of the life-style of its occupants, Louis XIV and his large family, which included the queen, his brother and his brother's second wife, certain cousins, Louis's children, his mistresses, their children by him, and eventually even his grandchildren, great-grandchildren and the spouses of all these. The queen and the Children of France, his legitimate and legitimized offspring, were entitled to attendants of high rank, many of whom also made claim to accommodation at Versailles. The proliferation of this huge family was certainly a fundamental reason for the transformation of the small hunting lodge of Louis XIII into a vast palace.

Furthermore, if the royal household stood at the centre of Versailles, the growth of the French government during Louis's reign, and his preference for Versailles as his permanent residence, necessitated the construction of a whole city of administrative buildings clustered around the château. From an artistic point of view, however, it was the needs of the king and the extended royal family which had the greatest potential influence on the architecture and arts at Versailles, since the royal life-style was considered to be directly related to the image of personal dignity and accomplishment (*gloire*) which was the principal goal of Louis's reign.

It seems appropriate to precede the history of the buildings and gardens of Versailles with some words about these individuals. In this context it is important to distinguish between those who were expected to accept whatever was offered by the king or his Buildings Office, and those who either were expected to or in fact did exert some personal influence on what was done, modifying if only subtly the absolute dominance of Louis's taste at Versailles.

First, however, a few general remarks on the character of Versailles, both as it was and as it now survives. It would be wrong to suggest that because Versailles was developed to meet the needs of a group of colourful personalities it was in any way a building which reflected their private tastes or eccentricities. It needs to be stressed that Versailles was a very formal, public place; only secondarily did it take on the characteristics of a private residence.

The relationship between the occupants and the environment created for them appears to be epitomized by the famous and possibly apocryphal exclamation of Madame de Maintenon, 'The symmetry, always the symmetry.' What this suggests is a rigid sense of taste and style imposed on those housed in the palace. The vast spaces and bare floors of the great apartments, particularly those decorated with brightly coloured, yet monumentally cold, marble and roofed with heavy gilt and painted ceilings, still make a very impersonal institutional impact. Though obviously Versailles was intended for living, the ambience is now, and probably always was, more suggestive of grandiose public buildings, such as the Houses of Parliament in London or the Capitol in Washington, than a private home, however magnificent. It is not correct to presume that it was only the ravages of the French Revolution and the conversion of Versailles into a museum which are responsible for the institutional atmosphere of the place today.

The state apartments of Versailles remained far more open than those of other countries.[2] The standard elements of a royal suite – guards' room, ante-chamber and chamber, and perhaps a small winter bedroom and private cabinet – were connected, with rooms having wide public access, unlike the royal apartments in England, which were rigidly aligned for privacy. The location of the king's bedroom at Versailles, only one room away from the Hall of Mirrors (see Fig. 6), troubled no one in France, but would not have been acceptable elsewhere. The entire court was on hand, formally dressed, from the moment of the king's ceremonial awakening in the morning until he equally ceremoniously retired near midnight. Even when he ate alone, which was the general practice at the Petit Couvert held in the first ante-chamber at night, the court and some outside visitors and tourists lined the walls and peered through open doorways from adjoining rooms. And Louis's family hour which followed the meal was held nearby in one of the cabinets behind the bedroom, but again with the doors flung wide so that all could see.

Since Louis XIV's taste was paramount at Versailles, it is with him that this discussion of the Versailles taste-makers must begin. From his mother, Anne of Austria, and Cardinal Mazarin, Louis had learned to live with a profusion of marvellous, precious things – jewels, gold and silver, fine furniture and works of art, particularly tapestries and paintings from both contemporaries and old masters. Mazarin's collection was a wonder of his age (and even a controversial political issue, as a minister's great wealth inevitably was). Louis was surrounded by parts of it in his formative years, and later inherited the entire collection. His mother seems to have fully shared the cardinal's tastes. A novelty was her splendid bathroom at the Louvre, indicating a concern for personal hygiene unusual in her century. It can hardly be considered a coincidence that four years after her death Louis undertook to build a luxurious bathroom for himself at Versailles (see Chapter 12). Anne and Mazarin surrounded themselves with extravagant examples of contemporary craftsmanship, such as metalwork and stone and wood inlays, and elaborate pieces of furniture which made spectacular use of such elements. In 1665, Sir Christopher Wren visited the newly redecorated old château at Versailles, and wrote to his brother:

> Not an inch within but is crouded with little Curiosities of Ornaments. The women, as they made here the Language and Fashions, and meddle with politics and philosophy, so they sway also in architecture; Works of Filgrand and little Knacks are in great Vogue; but Building certainly ought to have the Attribute of eternal, and therefore the only thing uncapable of new Fashions. The masculine furniture of Palais Mazarine pleas'd me much better . . .[3]

Wren also compared the exterior of Versailles to a rich livery, 'the mixtures of Brick, Stone, blue tile and Gold' apparently suggesting the comparison. He called the apartment of Anne at the Louvre glorious, speaking of its 'infinite rarities' and remarked that he saw it many times. Anne's and Mazarin's creations clearly were among the highlights of his visit to Paris, though it was four years after Mazarin's death. This 'parental' environment, now largely lost to us, must have held great sway over the imagination of the young Louis. The often told stories which suggest that the young king was ill housed at the beginning of his personal reign are misleading. Power, or at least the power of Anne's regency, must have been closely associated in his mind with the very richest sort of interior decor.

However, Louis certainly ignored the architecture of the regency. Though Anne's two new wings and handsome court within the medieval walls and towers of the castle of Vincennes (Fig. 19) are attractive, Vincennes was not in any way comparable to the great châteaux inherited by the king: Chambord, which returned to the crown in 1660, may well have been seen by the young man as a kind of reproach to the architecture of his mother's regency. At the least it demonstrated that a building could preserve the memory of the great achievements of monarchs.

Louis moved rapidly towards the grand scale of Chambord within the first decade of his personal reign, and there even seems to be evidence that he had already been impressed by grandiose architectural conceptions before the death of Mazarin and by the time of his wedding to Marie-Thérèse in 1660. The town and château of Richelieu (built by his father's great minister)

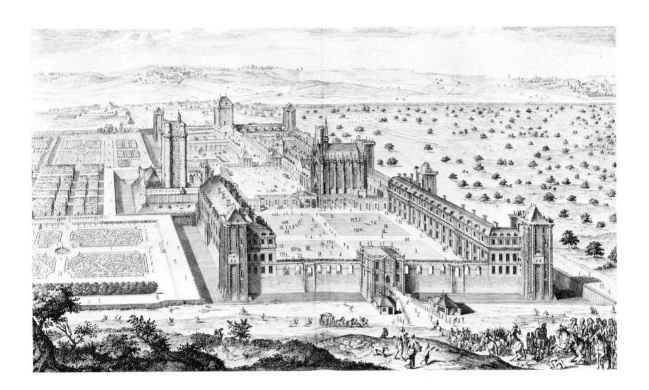

and the château of Cadillac, seen during that wedding trip, may have provided the inspiration for subsequent projects at Versailles and elsewhere.[4]

The most important single influence on Louis's attitude towards architecture was certainly the château of Vaux-le-Vicomte (Fig. 20), built in 1657–61
at a critical point in the king's life, precisely when, at the end of his
minority, he was forming his ideas on royal government. His finance minister, Nicolas Fouquet (1615–80), had recognized that the arts of architecture, garden design and painting could play a fundamental part in improving
and sustaining political power. Turning to the example of the two great
ministers, Cardinals Richelieu and Mazarin, Fouquet created a tangible
symbol of his own power by building a country residence for himself at
Vaux. He made use of the greatest artistic talents of the time, bringing
together Nicolas Poussin's most celebrated student, Charles Le Brun, and
two members of the king's artistic household, the gardener André Le Nôtre
and the architect Louis Le Vau. Fouquet provided them with the financial
wherewithal (largely from royal funds) for one of the great artistic colla-
borations of the century.

At Vaux Le Nôtre enlarged the traditions of the French formal garden
developed at Richelieu's residences. The result was a park of unprecedented

*19. P. Brissard: perspectival
view of the château of
Vincennes on the side with
the entry to the park
(south). Engraving*

grandeur and formality, suggesting that man could improve nature on a scale well beyond the confines of earlier gardens. Le Nôtre's garden was as much of an artistic statement as Le Vau's château, a fully realized dream of a setting worthy of the most wealthy and powerful of men.

20. Louis Le Vau and André Le Nôtre: château of Vaux-le-Vicomte, 1657-61

Le Vau's architecture was more traditional, but Le Brun's interiors rivalled the most sumptuous of contemporary Italian examples; the architect and painter planned interiors of exceptional comfort and practicality, making subtle but important adjustments to contemporary French taste. Vaux seemed to say that the best French design was of the highest international standard, second to none.

Fouquet's disgrace and imprisonment soon after he had displayed his new house to the king at a notoriously lavish fête (1661) leave no doubt that Louis learned, perhaps angrily, the political significance of the arts. Louis moved as quickly as circumstances and his means allowed to make extensive use of the artists who had worked for Fouquet. His monarchy then became a generous patron of the arts.

Louis's public person as described by contemporaries makes it easy to understand why grandeur as well as elegance increasingly characterized the royal demesne of Versailles. The Duke de Saint-Simon provides a vivid picture of a man who moved beyond the sumptuous on a moderate scale of his mother's world to the stupendous in the surroundings which he shaped for himself:

There was nothing equal to his bearing at reviews or indeed anywhere graced by the presence of ladies. I have already said that he had learned his gracious manner at his mother's court and in the drawing room of the Comtesse de Soissons ... He was sometimes gay, but never undignified, and never, at any time, did he do anything improper or indiscreet. His smallest gesture, his walk, bearing, and expression were all perfectly becoming, modest, noble, and stately, yet at the same time he always seemed perfectly natural. Added to which he had the immense advantage of a good figure, which made him graceful and relaxed ... On state occasions ... he looked so imposing that one had to become used to the sight of him if one were not to be exposed to the humiliation of breaking down or coming to a full stop ...[5]

In another passage Saint-Simon more directly addresses the issue of Louis's tastes and aims:

In everything he loved magnificently lavish abundance. He made it a principle from motives of policy and encouraged the court to imitate him; indeed, one way to win favour was to spend extravagantly on the table, clothes, carriages, buildings and gambling. For magnificence in such things he would speak to people ...

Louis's contemporaries were also awed by the fact that he did not seem to suffer physical discomfort as others did, especially that he hardly ever complained about the cold or bad weather. He hardly remarked rooms where water froze in basins. This certainly meant that creature comforts were considered secondary to visual impact in designs for him.

On the other hand he did enjoy many sensual pleasures of the environment. He treasured flowers and plants almost as much as works of art and surrounded himself with them. Hence the extraordinary creation of a room specifically made for the scent of exotic flowers at the Trianon de Porcelaine.

Louis in fact blended his mother's preferences for the amenities of refined urban life with his father's love of the hunt, and he attempted to create an environment for himself which included the best of both worlds. Saint-Simon also says: 'He loved the open air and exercise as long as strength was given to him ... all his life he was a superb horseman ...' He had a passion for stag hunting and shooting. It may be argued that one of the reasons for his eventual decision to make Versailles the principal royal residence was his desire to have the hunt and related country activities a part of his everyday life. But he was also the patron of the theatre, of Molière, and was on close terms with Racine.

The supreme creation of Louis XIV, Le Nôtre's great garden of Versailles, may well just stem from that, a fusion of aspects of the country with the urban environment. Louis restructured nature. Saint-Simon, in a particularly hostile mood, put it this way: 'It diverted him [Louis] to ride roughshod over nature and to use his money and ingenuity to subdue it to his will.' 'Who could help but be repelled and disgusted at the violences done to Nature? ...' The intention was most certainly to enhance nature – even, it has been argued by some more sympathetic to Louis's achievement, to humanize it.

Louis believed that France should be first in everything in Europe, and that her king should set the highest standards on all fronts. This attitude eventually caused him to try to move beyond the creation of the best in the arts according to contemporary standards and to set new standards in both the quality and the quantity of what he built.

The queen, Marie-Thérèse, was a bland, retiring and dutiful personality who exerted little influence on court taste. It is difficult to discern any special interests she may have had which may have been significant, except for her exceptional religiousness. She seems to have enjoyed dressing as a nun at times and was meticulous about observing her many daily devotions, but she also had no objections to living in style. In matters of taste, as in most things, she was absolutely deferential to Louis. It is not certain if she was often even consulted. The new Versailles palace was planned in 1669 almost as two separate entities, one for the king, the other for his wife; both areas were similarly decorated.[6]

The role of Louis's mistresses in the history of Versailles has always, and rightly, been stressed. However, the influence of his first love, Louise de La Vallière, on the amenities planned for the château was relatively small; little was specifically built for her. But, as Saint-Simon said, 'The awkward situation of his mistresses and the dangers involved in conducting such scandalous affairs in a busy capital, crowded with people of every kind of mentality, played no small part in deciding him to leave [Paris for Versailles], for he was embarrassed by the crowds whenever he went in or out or appeared upon the streets.' 'The liaison with Mademoiselle de La Vallière, which was at first kept secret, occasioned many excursions to Versailles ...' It is also clear that it was of importance to Louis that Versailles had been the scene of the most exquisite moments of this romance.

The influence of Madame de Montespan, the successor to La Vallière, was considerable. One story about Montespan may serve to illustrate how very different she was. Louis decided to build her a discreet hideaway a stone's throw from Versailles on the other side of the Pool of Clagny. When Montespan saw the designs which Antoine Le Pautre produced for the building, she remarked 'This would only be fit for a girl from the opera!'[7] Montespan was a Mortemart, a family which jokingly referred to Louis's Bourbon roots as *parvenu*. She obviously felt her position to be that of a second and possibly more adequate queen. She certainly felt entitled to a similarly regal life-style, just outside the public spotlight. Clagny became the symbol of the role she saw herself playing, the exquisite retreat of an enchantress (see Fig. 85).

But Madame de Montespan's actual role as an arbiter of taste is not easy to determine. There is no doubt that she was a clever and amusing woman such as the king confessed he preferred, but what we know of the details of Clagny and the slightly earlier Versailles apartment by the king's staircase is not very revealing of whether she had only veto power or some individual taste. Madame de Montespan certainly at times patronized the arts and in particular supported the work of an establishment which produced fine embroidery, the best example of which was a hanging for the throne room at Versailles preserved only by a drawing (Fig. 21), but whether she did more than give some financial support to the craftspeople in this is not clear.

Other members of the royal family with greater position were expected to demonstrate both high standards of taste and a certain individuality. Unfortunately the major monument to the taste of Monsieur, Louis's only brother, the château of Saint Cloud, was burned in the nineteenth century. Monsieur was certainly encouraged to patronize artists not employed at Versailles, such as Mignard, who, when he first returned from Italy, painted a famous ceiling for the gallery at Saint Cloud. The official guide to Versailles by the Sieur Combes (1681) actually digresses to discuss this wonder, suggesting that it was a glory for the family.

Fortunately we know more about the situation of Monseigneur, Louis the dauphin, the king's only surviving legitimate child. He was urged, perhaps even forced, to become an independent patron of the arts. His apartment at Versailles (on the ground floor facing south and west) was much visited. The Boulle cabinet there was one of the most admired parts of the palace, and Monseigneur's art collection was often mentioned. The independence shown by him in the decoration of his private residence at Meudon is also established. His decorators were not those usually used at Versailles. Monseigneur seems to have had up-to-date, even forward-looking tastes, perhaps enjoying grace more than grandeur.

Some designs survive for the apartments at Versailles of Louis's legitimized children. Their share in the creation of these designs is impossible to establish. But they appear to have played at best a minor part, since many of the drawings remain with the papers of the King's Buildings Office. It would, however, be interesting to know whether the attempt by the king to

Meuble Brodé dans la Sale d'Audience de l'Apartement a Versailles

establish his bastards in the succession to the throne meant that their role in the shaping of taste was eventually modelled on that of the dauphin. There is some evidence that the Duke and Duchess of Maine had such pretensions.

The dominant female figure of the reign after 1683 was Madame de Maintenon, Louis's last mistress and probably his morganatic wife. All of the surviving indications are that she had very little interest in Versailles. She concentrated her attentions instead on the school she established and built for impoverished young noble ladies at Saint Cyr. The famous literary connections of Saint Cyr with Racine apparently had no visual equivalent. Her apartment at Versailles hardly aspired to any special artistic interest, though, of course, since the king spent much time there, its furnishings must have been fine.

Marie-Adélaïde of Savoy, the wife of Louis's grandson, the Duke of Burgundy, and the mother of Louis XV, is the last royal figure who may have influenced the design of Louis's Versailles. In 1696 the young duchess of twelve transformed family life there. A little charmer, she quickly won the heart of the king and of Madame de Maintenon as well. So important did this little girl become that the king took her for a walk every day. And he tried to please her, in spite of the great shortage of money during the 1690s. He provided a charming place for her to play at the Ménagerie (zoo), which was beautifully redecorated. This new decor was outstanding in originality and quality and was an important harbinger of the eighteenth century (see Chapter 13). Marie-Adélaïde's presence and the dauphin's taste paved the way for the style of the new century in France; but in all likelihood Louis's architects were developing a lighter, gayer style on their own. It quickly permeated all the new designs, from the king's bedroom of 1701 to the grand new chapel, two places where charm was hardly called for.

21 (opposite). Meuble brodé dans la Salle d'Audience de l'Appartement à Versailles (*T.H.C. 1554*). *Coloured drawing*

MONEY

The funds for Versailles came from the treasury. The fiscal administration was thus a basic element in the creation of the palace. Colbert was thus the ideal superintendent of the King's Buildings Office, being minister of finance and responsible for building, the national economy and the collection of taxes.

The principal elements of the tax structure which fed the royal treasury hardly changed during Louis's long reign. Increases in revenue depended entirely on two factors. The first was the efficient collection of the sums due. The second was the stimulation of the national economy so that larger taxes would be owed. Colbert proceeded on both of these fronts and was quite successful, particularly during the 1660s.[8]

His attempt to stimulate the national economy is famous. His policy carries the name of 'mercantilism' and is often seen as an important early experiment in a controlled economy. The essential element of his programme was the idea that the economic interests of the nation as a whole were more important than those of individuals or parts of the kingdom. This justified an increase in the power of the central administration. A balance of exports over imports, with a consequent accumulation of bullion, was considered fundamental to economic development. Colbert attempted to implement this policy by the imposition of additional customs duties and the stimulation of industries oriented to export. Though a heavy price was eventually paid in international relations for this protectivism, in its early days the mercantile system operated at a profit, particularly as far as the government coffers were concerned.

The foundation of the royal manufactories, of which the Gobelins tapestry and furniture works is the most famous, is a consequence of mercantilism which was, coincidentally, of great importance to the history of Versailles. Originally established by Colbert to produce goods which would be in demand abroad by setting high standards of craftsmanship in the decorative arts, these institutions were set to furnish the royal houses. Versailles became a vast showroom of the best luxury items to come out of the government workshops. And the French bought at home rather than from abroad, restraining the traditional cash outflow for luxury goods.

A related development, with a similar result in terms of its economic impact and its effect on the appearance of Versailles, was the opening of French quarries for ornamental marbles and stones, most of which had previously come from Italy.

For twenty years or so it appeared that the wealth of France, the richest and most populous country in Europe at the time (with about twenty million people), could support both the greatest military power in Europe and the construction of splendid monuments to a regime which was aware of its duties to science and the arts.

Thus in its early years Versailles was the product of an economic mentality which had an almost euphoric sense that nearly anything was possible. However, in the actual building history of the palace this point of view prevailed for less than twenty years, or about thirty per cent of the time this history covers.

The period when most of the construction of the gardens and the palace was actually realized saw a more reserved optimism. While there may have been confidence that eventually vast amounts could be raised, at most times there were important limitations. The quality sought was not just the production of prodigious things but also keeping within budgets. The question must often have been how to achieve the maximum with the available, substantial but limited, resources. The frequent re-using of existing elements, from walls to doorways and panelling, testifies to this.

The other factor which had most influence on the ebb and flow of projects conceived and built was the military. Colbert stated that building came second to military triumph for the king's *gloire*. The royal accounts make it clear that the state of war or peace had the most direct effect on the availability of funds, even well before the desperate days of the end of the reign.

The relationship between military demands and the funds available for Versailles is shown by the table of expenses for the château drawn up by Marinier, Hardouin-Mansart's clerk, in 1691 (Table overleaf). It shows the expenses for Versailles for each year after 1663.

Expenditure increased substantially during the four years of peace which followed the War of Devolution (1664–7). This spending, one might argue, was the result of the good times brought about by the Treaty of Aix-la-Chapelle. It was during the period from 1668 to 1672 that Versailles as we know it emerged, a grandiose gesture of the king and his government. The importance of the Aix treaty for Versailles lay in direct financial benefits

TABLE 1: MARINIER'S TABLE OF ANNUAL EXPENSES
FOR THE CHÂTEAU OF VERSAILLES

(1691; from Pierre Clément (ed.), *Lettres, Instructions et Mémoires de Colbert*, Vol. V, Paris, 1868)

DÉPENSES DU CHASTEAU DE VERSAILLES

1664	834,037^l 2^s 6^d			REPORT	19,553,003^l 13^s 8^d		
1665	783,673	4		1678	2,622,655	3	10
1666	526,954	7		1679	5,667,331	17	
1667	214,300	18		1680	5,839,761	19	8
1668	618,006	5	7	1681	3,854,382	2	
1669	1,238,375	7		1682	4,235,123	8	7
1670	1,996,452	12	4	1683	3,714,572	5	V11
1671	3,396,595	12	6	1684	5,762,092	2	8
1672	2,802,718	1	5	1685	11,314,281	10	10
1673	847,004	3	10	1686	6,558,210	7	9
1674	1,384,269	10	3	1687	5,400,245	18	
1675	1,933,755	8	1	1688	4,551,596	16	2
1676	1,348,222	10	10	1689	1,710,055	10	
1677	1,628,638	11	4	1690	368,101	10	1
A REPORTER	19,553,003^l 13^s 8^d			TOTAL	81,151,414^l 9^s 2^d		

and in the future potential it seemed to express for a prosperous state. The 'glorious' peace certainly determined the large scale of the enterprise. Expenditure in 1671 (see Table 1) was more than fifteen times that of the war year of 1667 and, even more significantly, more than six times that of the earlier peaceful year of 1666.

The momentum gathered in these postwar years was enough to keep Versailles growing even in the face of major military action and related financial difficulties which came with the war against the Dutch of 1672. The Marinier chart (Table 1) correctly shows that the new war produced drastic cutbacks in 1673, but these were only to a level higher than that of any year before 1668.

In 1674, though war was fully under way, the allocation of funds for Versailles was substantially increased, and it remained at a high level for the rest of the war. This pattern is particularly striking when it is remembered that it was only the finishing touches to the château which remained to be done.

After the Treaties of Nijmegen (1678-9) and the peace, expenditure rose by nearly a million in 1678, then by three million more in 1679. This last increase is almost equal to the *total expenses* for the previous high year of 1671.

The need to keep busy a large standing army during the peacetime of the 1680s accelerated work on projects where the army could be involved. Such a momentum of truly extravagant projects built up that a jump in expenditure occurred during 1685 which nearly doubled the already fabulous figure of the previous year. Even the king was staggered by these outlays, and a dramatic reduction was effected for 1686, 1687 and 1688, though the reduced budgets remained enormous by the standards of the 1670s.

The formation of the League of Augsburg by Louis's enemies and the outbreak of a new war with most of Europe lined up against France is reflected in the final entries on the Marinier chart for 1689 and 1690. It was no longer a question of diverting some funds from ongoing projects and postponing the undertaking of new ones; there was a grave crisis which threatened the regime. It rapidly became clear that tax income could not meet even the basic military needs, and, further, that money could not be borrowed to meet the national emergency, much less to continue work on Versailles. At first the honouring of commitments previously made and a related desire to suggest that things were in fact not so very grave kept some work going, but by 1693 the money ran out.

Even the Peace Treaty of Rijswijk in September 1697 failed to produce much of an immediate improvement. But gradually, with some sense of a possible normal future, a few projects were undertaken as the end of the century approached.

France again was plunged into a terrible war after the death of Charles II of Spain in 1700, but surprisingly this did not destroy all of the small momentum built up during the few years of peace. The building of the Versailles chapel, a grandiose undertaking, continued. It was begun before the year of the opening of hostilities, but its decoration and construction continued through the most dreadful moments of this long war, which lasted until the Treaties of Utrecht were signed in April 1713. Some bravado certainly showed in this, and the financing proved very difficult.

This gesture by Louis towards the completion of his great palace clearly demonstrates that by the end of the reign Versailles had become a special symbol for both the king and the world, one whose value could no longer be counted just in ordinary financial terms. Its importance after 1670 as a symbol of the achievements of the reign meant that Versailles was often able to compete favourably even with the military for limited funds. Architecture was not always the first to suffer.

One last economic factor must be mentioned. For approximately thirty years from about 1680 to about 1710 Europe was living through a little Ice Age. The memoirist Dangeau was not at all surprised that a Christmas season was celebrated with sleigh rides and skating on the canal. And construction at Versailles was occasionally brought to a halt by deep frost in early November.

The most important effect of the inclement weather was indirect. In spite of Colbert's efforts, France remained an agricultural country. Crop failures caused by early and late frosts reduced health, popular morale, and taxes, and thus had an influence on the history of Versailles. The combination of heavy taxation and under-production of food increasingly crippled France. Good weather might have made an important difference to the royal finances during the 1690s and the early 1700s. Increased prosperity would certainly have had an effect on the relatively meagre final years of Louis XIV's Versailles, and the history of Louis's château might not have ended, as it did, with uncharacteristic modesty.

THE ENCHANTED
PALACE

(1664–8)

'This is a château that might be called an enchanted palace ... perfect.'
So wrote the author of the *Fête of the Enchanted Isle*, which first drew
public attention to Versailles. 'It charms in all possible ways ...' The writer
of 1664 remarked that the king, wishing to give his mother, wife and the
whole court

the pleasure of some special festivities in a setting possessed of all the qualities
which a country house might allow to be admired, chose Versailles at four leagues
from Paris ... Everything smiles without as within. Gold and marble rival in their
beauty and brilliance. And while it does not have the vastness which is to be found
in some of the other palaces of His Majesty, everything is so highly finished, so
well laid out, so well cared for, that nothing is the equal of it. Its symmetry, the
richness of its furnishings, the beauty of its walks and the infinite number of its
flowers, as well as of its orange trees, make the surroundings of this spot especially
extraordinary.'

Some critics were less sure of the perfection nature had bestowed on the
spot; they expressed openly the opinion that Versailles was a poor place for
a house. Louis's frequent detractor, the Duke de Saint-Simon, described it
thus: ' ... that most dismal and thankless of spots, without vistas, woods
or water, without soil even, for all the surrounding land is quicksand or
bog, and the air cannot be healthy.'

The château inherited by Louis XIV from his father was a modest affair,
not in any way worthy even of the description of 1664. Because of the fine
hunting in the area, Louis XIII had begun by buying some bits and pieces
of land. By 1624 he felt his holdings substantial enough to build a small
lodge to stay overnight. Of it little is known, but Saint-Simon immortalized
it as the 'little house of cards'. The marshal of Bassompierre, in his memoirs
of 1627, wrote that it would be impossible to reproach Louis XIII for his
'puny' château in which a simple gentleman could hardly take much pride.

An inventory of the royal apartment of 1630 survives which describes the king as lodged in four modest rooms simply furnished and hung with tapestries. It also mentions a small gallery decorated with paintings of the siege of La Rochelle.

It was not, however, this 'little card house' which Louis XIV inherited. It had been pulled down and replaced by a second château, whose history is better documented than that of the first. Contracts with LeRoy for the new building span the years 1631-4. It was built of red brick and white stone, with a slate roof, materials then often used for moderately important buildings. During the 1630s the king acquired from the Gondi family the nearby village and various other properties, including Trianon; this made possible the creation of the park of Versailles.

The gardens undertaken in 1639 by Mollet and Masson, which replaced an earlier design by Menours and Boyceau of uncertain date, were apparently quite impressive, and might even have established the broad lines of the garden of Louis XIV. This château is shown in a charming engraving by Silvestre of the central section seen from the garden side on the west

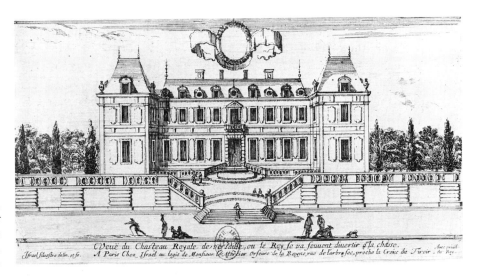

22a. Israel Silvestre: view of the royal château of Versailles. Engraving from the series Maisons Royales, 1652

(Fig. 22a). The artist had such a modest impression of the building that he even reduced by two the number of windows on this side. A surviving ground plan (Fig. 22b) shows an unpretentious *corps de logis* containing a vestibule (or central salon) and four rooms extended somewhat by two cabinets contained in semi-detached corner towers. Four additional rooms and two stairways were included in a pair of wings extending towards the east which together with the *corps de logis* enclosed a central courtyard.

There is nothing to suggest that the château was considered to be of much importance during the long minority of Louis XIV. A brief period of use for some royal dinners is documented in 1651, but on the whole the place assumed so unimportant a place in the life of the minority that it is almost surprising to find Versailles in Silvestre's series of prints of the royal residences.

While there is little to substantiate the romantic tale that Louis rediscovered an overgrown and cobweb-covered Versailles while hunting with his young wife shortly after his assumption of personal rule in 1661, a period of some neglect must have suggested the urgent need for refurbishing if the building were to be used at all.

In line with the ambitious character of the 1660s, the restoration of Versailles was done in a very grand manner, such as almost to efface the memory of the original. The words of Colbert give some idea of the scale. In a letter to the king he said: ' . . . if your Majesty should wish to find out where the more than 500.000 *écus* are which have been spent on Versailles in the last two years, you will certainly have difficulty finding them.'[10] And these substantial moneys were not being spent on a new château; in that context they seem enormous.

The renovations did include the construction of several buildings, but most probably the chief devourer of money was the moving of vast quantities of earth. Of the new structures, the Orangery, with large south-facing windows, was the largest (Fig. 23). It was excavated into the hillside below the south side of the château. Bernini admired it in September 1665[11] and thought it attractive enough to recommend that it be frescoed in grisaille inside so that it could be used for court activities during the warm months when the orange trees were moved outside. The Orangery had above it a large level terrace which was planted in the elaborate form of a *parterre en broderie*.

Another innovation with a somewhat similar function was the Ménagerie (zoo), with various apartments furnished to allow for relaxation: one was arranged for dining while looking down into the large open yards in which the collections of birds and animals were kept (Fig. 24).

The eastern approach to the château itself was redesigned. Three great avenues were traced and lined with trees. Terracing was undertaken to make the immediate approach more regular and gradual, and a new forecourt for the château was created by the construction of a pair of rectangular buildings to serve as kitchens and stables.

For Louis XIII Versailles had been a retreat to which he could retire with his closest friends after the hunt. The renovations of the early 1660s indicate that Louis XIV planned visits with a far more numerous court. The large size of the new kitchen, occupying an entire separate building located to the

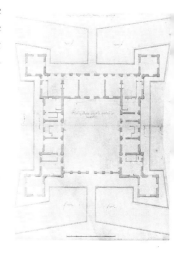

22b. Plan of the ground floor of the château of Versailles. Drawing, before 1662

23. Adam-François Van der Meulen: view of the château and Orangery of Versailles seen from the south (Satory hill) (M.V. 725).
Painting, 1664

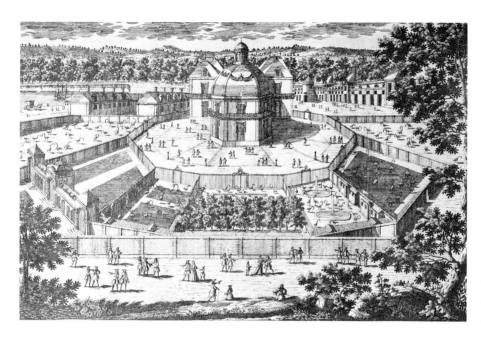

24. Aveline: view of the salon and grotto of the zoo (Ménagerie) and some of the cages

north-east of the principal court of the château, suggests that it may have been planned to accommodate outdoor festivities as well as ordinary meals.

Colbert did not consider Versailles to be excessively grand: 'This house has much more to do with the pleasure and the entertainment of Your Majesty than with your *gloire* . . .', he remarked.[12] Yet Louis lavished attention on his small house: he added an iron balcony around the upper floor of the building, gilded like many ornaments of the roof, and he transformed the interior apartments into *Wunderkammern* of furnishings and *objets d'art*. Wren, who came in the wake of the fame spread by the descriptions of the 1664 *fête*, reacted strongly against what he saw, but his remarks give an indication of the lavish interior renovations.[13] (See Chapter 3, p. 40.)

Little has survived of the Versailles interiors of the 1660s which could either substantiate Wren's criticism or vindicate the young king. Three years later La Fontaine and Mademoiselle de Scudéry both found the rooms superb, but then they saw them perhaps at a more perfect moment, and they were both more or less official apologists of the king. The single surviving element of that decoration, though not without charm, would on balance seem to sustain Wren's criticism. Louis's gallery of portraits of the beauties of the court, begun shortly after 1660, but completed between 1664 and 1665 and then installed at Versailles, consisted of thirty or more pictures which were commissioned from the Beaubrun brothers. The style of the painters was at the time slightly dated and their abilities were somewhat

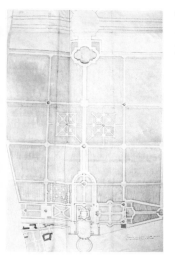

25. Plan original du Chasteau et Petit Parc de Versailles comme il esté Enciennement avant que le Roy y est fait travailler. *Coloured drawing, c. 1664*

declining, as the more than twenty portraits still at Versailles in the Apartment of Madame de Maintenon show. Whatever the effect of the group of pictures as originally installed, they suggest that the taste of the king at that moment was turned more towards pretty faces and elegant society than towards high art.

The probable state of the gardens in 1664 is best-known from a large plan at the Bibliothèque de l'Institut (Fig. 25). It shows large parterres extending out on three sides from the château towards the park. The smallest of these covered more than twice the area of the château, and the arrangement suggests that each was designed to relate to one of the façades of the building.

The three parterres were quite different from each other in shape and character. That to the north (right on the plan) had highly developed waterworks, that to the south featured flowerbeds, and that to the west (above on the plan) was apparently planted with lawn. There may even have been a scheme to represent three of the four elements, namely water, earth and fire, with the flowerbeds evoking the sun and the grass earth, but this is difficult to prove.

What is most striking about this scheme is the lack of integration of the area surrounding the château with the park as a whole.[14] Most of the park was simply left covered by natural woods. It is arguable that Le Nôtre deliberately reduced the relationship between the woody areas and the parterres in an ingenious attempt to create an effect of regularity around the château and to hide the extremely irregular character of the site. In any event he produced a design quite different from his earlier works such as Vaux-le-Vicomte (see Fig. 20).

Le Nôtre's treatment of the western grass parterre is typical. He gave it the enclosed form of a traditional architectural shape, the basilica: the rectangular parterre sloped gently downhill and terminated in a graceful curve, not as it might appear at first glance with a semicircular wall of trees, but with a balustraded terrace with a central stairway; the terrace was surrounded by two large curved ramps descending from the level of the parterre to the much lower level of the bottom of the stairway. With this system of terrace and ramps Le Nôtre both created an enclosure and provided an attractive transition to the park beyond, which was after all the main reason for the existence of the château. He also solved an important functional problem of the western area. It was from the west that the royal hunt gained access to the great park of Versailles. The area below had previously been difficult of access and impossible for the carriages which frequently accompanied the hunt. The ramps were useful and also provided an attractive terminus to the parterre.

A delightful discovery awaited those who walked to the bottom of the parterre: a broad *allée* below the terrace which terminated with a high jet of water. There can be no doubt, however, from this aspect of the design, that the lower park was seen as an entirely different entity from that immediately adjacent to the château. Le Nôtre was operating at his most creative here, in spite of the limitations of the land, which prevented the making of a tour de force such as the great vista at Vaux-le-Vicomte.

The history of the *fête* of 1664 itself explains the mentality of a second, very different phase of planning which eventually transformed Louis's modest house described above. Like the work at Versailles, the party started modestly, then grew rapidly beyond recognition.

Louis had the idea that his court would be amused by an entertainment built around the idea of a lottery in which all the tickets would prove good. The ladies were to receive jewellery. But the *fête* ended as an extravaganza including events of horsemanship, banquets, plays by Molière, music by Lully, and a vast final tableau in which Armida's enchanted island was destroyed by a fireworks display. Ariosto's witch Armida held the court in her power for the three days, as she had the knight Roland; then at the end – with the spectacular conclusion – her power came to an end and the court could move on.

The joys of this *fête* were not to be just for the privileged few who were invited or who, uninvited, watched from a discreet distance. The whole world was informed of every detail, first, of course, by the *Gazette*, then by a printed account in the form of a short book. Finally, an enormous enterprise of the drawing and engraving of many large plates made the *fête* one of the best-known parties of the century. It may be that more recherché entertainments took place elsewhere (the Medicis at Florence come to mind), but Louis created a vast apparatus of publicity, to which the fame of Versailles owes more than a little: the *fête* publications played a fundamental role in the accelerated development of the royal retreat.

The success of the *fête* certainly hastened development of the gardens. In September 1665, when Bernini arrived for his visit, the first Versailles of Louis XIV had been substantially destroyed by ambitious new projects. While Bernini found the area above and beyond the new Orangery (that is, south of the château) in good shape, he stated that Le Nôtre had been obliged to explain to him just what was going on in other important areas, namely to the west and the north. Several of these changes involved financial commitments unthinkable two years earlier.

The development of the western axis was the most impressive and expensive. The dimensions of the first parterre remained basically the same, but a vast new system of ramps was developed which allowed the creation of

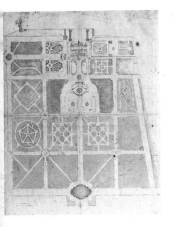

a second parterre farther down the hill. This development of the park is shown on a plan at the Bibliothèque Nationale (Fig. 26).

Soon the decision must have been made to proceed at whatever cost to create the most striking possible setting for the château. The Versailles gardens then began to assume the spectacular grandeur and scale for which they are now so famous.

A simultaneous development was that certain new features of the park began to spell out the propaganda of the glory of the reign. The Grotto of Thetis begun in 1666 might have been built to tell precisely why Versailles had been created. Mademoiselle de Scudéry conveyed its message in 1668: '[the king] goes [to Versailles] from time to time to relax and put aside for a moment his great and illustrious [but] tiring duties . . . [It does not prevent]

26. Plan of the Versailles park showing the ground plans of the structures built for the fête of 1668. Coloured drawing

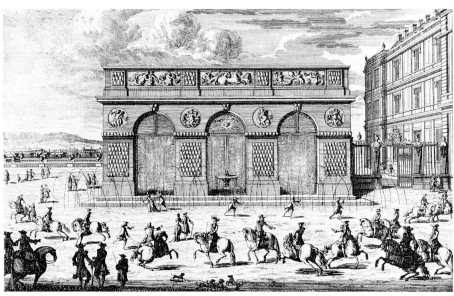

27. Perelle: the Grotto of Thetis. Engraving, before 1670

his prompt return to work with the same fervour as that with which the sun begins to illumine the world when he rises from the waters where he has rested himself.' The exterior reliefs depicted the descent of Apollo into the sea, while the grille showed the rays of the setting sun shining on the six parts of the world (Fig. 27). Inside, life-sized sculptures showed Apollo, seated, served by the muses (Fig. 45); on either side his horses, also full-sized, were unharnessed and cared for by attendants. Thetis, in whose home Apollo finds himself, is not shown. To contemporaries the resting sun god represented Louis, since the king's device was the sun, and Versailles was where he refreshed himself for his great actions.

28. Jean-Baptist Tuby: Apollo rising from the sea. Versailles, the Basin of Apollo

Soon afterwards this solar imagery was completed by another monument, still preserved *in situ*. Tuby's monumental sculptures in the basin at the foot of the western slope on the main axis show Apollo rising from the sea, refreshed and embarking upon his daily work (Fig. 28).

Another important site was decorated contemporarily with sculptures which made direct political points and developed the same Apollo theme. The lower western parterre was given a clever fountain by the Marsy brothers representing the story of Latona (Fig. 29), which may well have had a personal meaning for Louis. He and his mother, regent during his minority, had suffered and then risen above the mocking of the common crowd during the civil uprising in the 1650s called the Fronde. Latona,

29. Pierre Le Pautre: the Fountain of Latona. Engraving after the sculptures of the Marsy brothers, 1678

mother of Apollo, had been taunted by the Lycian peasants, who were eventually punished by Zeus and changed into various low creatures such as frogs.[15] The theme of *lèse-majesté* was thus introduced, but with charm, since the Latona theme had an aquatic aspect which made it ideal for a fountain.

Le Nôtre was then stimulated further to develop a stupendous western axis for the garden. The *allée* descending from the Latona parterre to the basin where Tuby's Apollo in his chariot rose from the waters was much widened, and the Academy of Science was set to work planning a great canal which eventually prolonged the axis for miles.

But by creating this tour de force in the history of gardening, Le Nôtre posed an extremely awkward problem for the King's Buildings Office. The garden, which was devouring enormous sums for construction, decoration and planting, also created the need for an entirely new residence to provide an adequate centrepiece for such a grand setting.

Louis and Colbert apparently wrestled with this problem for some years. It is unlikely that they were willing to move towards any kind of solution until plans for the finishing of the Louvre were completed in 1667, but from that point the rebuilding of the château of Versailles must have seemed inevitable. Progress towards a decision was not quick, even then, however, for a number of good reasons. In the first place, the royal building programme was over-extended. Louis was simultaneously restoring the Tuileries to serve as a temporary Paris residence while the new Louvre was

30. Cross-section and elevations for additions to the old château of Versailles (C.C. 271). Drawing, 1668 or before

under way, redecorating apartments at Saint Germain-en-Laye and at Chambord, and continuing the vast works of the Versailles gardens.

A well-known drawing in Stockholm (Fig. 30) is in fact an early project for the rebuilding of the château, and is of significance since it must be inferred from it that a plan just to alter and expand the old château was seriously entertained alongside the alternative of creating a splendid new palace.[16] However, for a time until about 1667, while the design of the garden was the major concern at Versailles, the issue of the new palace was kept pending.

In 1668, in spite of the transitional state of affairs, Louis decided to take full credit for what he had accomplished, even if it was fragmented. Important writers such as La Fontaine, author of the *Fables*, and Mademoiselle de Scudéry were encouraged to turn their talents to the celebration of Versailles. The painter Patel was paid to record both what had been done and the appearance that the western axis of the garden would have after the completion of the canal (Fig. 31). Louis even gave another *fête* as opulent as that of 1664. Silvestre made impressive engravings of it, since Louis wanted the world to know of the artistic accomplishments of his court and the increasing brilliance of his designers and to show his apparently limitless financial resources.

Mademoiselle de Scudéry's book, written at the end of 1668, first evokes the enchanted palace she has visited in words not very different in tone and meaning from those written to describe the *fête* of 1664; but then she boldly

31 Pierre Patel: the great bird's-eye view of the château and park of Versailles of 1668, a view from the east (M.V. 765)

32. *The Cour de Marbre, château of Versailles, modern view from the east*

states that in a few months' time so much would have changed that a visitor would hardly recognize the place. This can only be a reference to the fact that work was finally to get under way on a new palace.

Louis could never bring himself to knock down the little brick château. He certainly considered the possibility, and he fully realized that the continued existence of the brick château compromised, even marred, the important eastern façade. He was aware that the structure impressed no one, yet he never accepted any of the projects proposed as replacements. Studies have shown that it was necessary to take down and rebuild this modest building almost completely a few years later, but Louis actually did so rather than to lose it.

The original courtyard of the red brick château is still visible (Fig. 32). In 1683 Louis chose to sleep within the old walls, and he died in his bedroom there in 1715. In function and in fact the château of the 1660s remained at the centre of the great palace which enveloped it and rendered it obsolete.

It has been argued that filial piety preserved the old château. Certainly this was one reason. But this small building was also Louis's enchanted palace, the point of departure for the development of the uniquely magnificent park and lovely outbuildings. That fact surely provided the main motivation.

THE

ENVELOPPE

(1668–74)

1668 must have seemed a banner year. The successful completion of the War of Devolution added a sense of achievement to the young king's presumptions of pre-eminence. The time was at hand for grand gestures; and this mentality determined the course of events at Versailles.

The King's Buildings Office had proved itself capable of great works with the triumphant resolution of the problems of the design of a new Louvre a year before, and Colbert's other projects, such as the redecoration of the interior of the Tuileries, were proceeding well. The critical acclaim which greeted the designs of the Louvre must have been particularly gratifying. What Colbert achieved there was nothing less than a demonstration that his team could produce a palace superior to one designed by the great Bernini. For the first time since the Renaissance it seemed that French royal architects could rival the Italians, who were credited as being unsurpassed in all the arts.

The first issue at Versailles was clearly whether to knock down the château of brick and to build an entirely new building worthy of the spectacular park, or simply to make additions. Louis clearly understood that there was a serious conflict between the priorities of sentiment and the necessity of doing something to reflect the political pretensions of his regime.

At first it appears to have been sentiment which gained the day, and during the last months of 1668 and the first of 1669 work proceeded on a scheme which Colbert called the Enveloppe. The old château was preserved and surrounded by a new palace along the general lines indicated in an elevation (Fig. 30). During these months three walls rose around the old château to a height of about twenty feet, and the arcade of the gallery below the terrace was largely completed. But, as Charles Perrault tells us, the new palace failed to please the king, and work on it was halted in June of 1669.

Then in the triumphant spirit of the time the decision was made to proceed with an entirely new palace and to replace the old. Several leading French architects submitted projects. Colbert's comments on the plans of the theatre designer Vigarani, Gabriel, the sieur P., and Louis Le Vau have survived. The remarks of Colbert are, as was usual for him, to the point, and sometimes highly critical. However, grand elements are often singled out for praise and nowhere is anyone criticized for thinking in terms of a truly enormous palace. A country residence parallel in its scale to the great new Louvre was certainly what the superintendent and the king desired. The design by Louis Le Vau was preferred and possibly accepted.

A drawing in the collection of the Stockholm Nationalmuseum seems to be the plan of the ground floor of the Le Vau project criticized by Colbert (Fig. 33). This gives a good idea of the kind of building and the size of the structure that it was decided to undertake. The drawing also indicates the

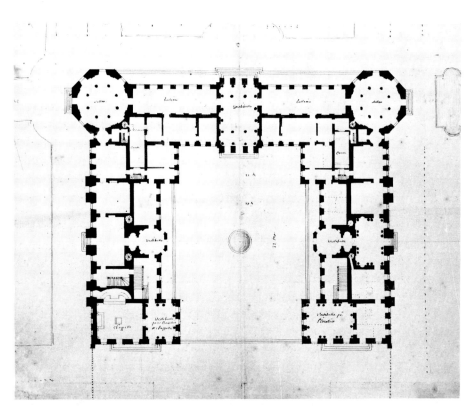

33. Workshop of Louis Le Vau: project for a new palace for Versailles (T.H.C. 3292), detail. Drawing

intended fate of the old château: most of it was to be left standing while the construction went on, and after the completion of the new palace it was to be pulled down to open up a monumental forecourt.

The three newly built walls were to be respected, though, oddly, it was the back side of the garden arcade which was to serve as a central element of the new façade of 1669. Le Vau's grand new scheme called for a sub-stantial expansion of the Enveloppe towards the west and most notably the addition of vast pavilions and galleries (at the top of Fig. 33). Other changes were not more modest, great stairways and vestibules being added between the north and south walls of the Enveloppe project. Colbert says that the king made a 'great and public declaration' of his decision to destroy the old château, in the heady atmosphere of these months.

Louis's action was, however, premature. For reasons which remain un-clear, by the end of 1669 and in spite of the slight embarrassment involved, he reversed his decision; the great plan was aborted and still another project was rapidly drawn up, this one returning definitively to the idea of the Enveloppe.[17] Versailles had been on the brink of becoming a grand monu-ment, a full response to the great park Le Nôtre was in the process of fashioning. Suddenly it was restored to what it had been in 1668, a more modest place of retreat for the king to visit to recover from the fatigue of his governmental responsibilities.

This retrenchment was not easy to bring about, however necessary it may have been; and there is no question that the task with which the architects were faced was complex and demanding. An important problem arose from the decision to abandon the grandiose ceremonial areas, galleries and salons of Le Vau's great project. Interior spaces had to be redefined in a much more limited area to provide these lost amenities, yet in such a manner as to hide completely any suggestion that the plans had been simplified, since retrenchment was not suitable to the pretensions of the king.

It is unfortunate that we have no information about the formulation of the plan which was eventually accepted. Tradition has always assigned to Le Vau the credit for the building which was completed. But we do not know whether there was a committee of compromise, as there had been for the Louvre, which hammered out the final project.

What is clear is that the palace which was eventually completed was unusual both in the circumstances of its creation and in the manner of its planning. First in the order of priorities seems to have come the creation of the three adequately grand garden elevations for the building. The second task was the reorganizing of the interior spaces.

Many points remained open to discussion for a number of years. Debate on the basic form of the stairway leading to the king's apartment eventually spanned five or six years. Long after the roof was up in 1670, projects were still being seriously considered which would have radically transformed im-portant interior spaces in terms both of form and of function (see Fig. 111).

Since the whole undertaking of a new palace was certainly the result of Le Nôtre's splendid park, the need was clearly for a building which would

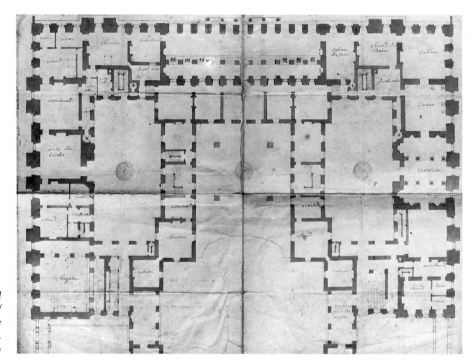

34. Plan of the ground floor of the palace of Versailles including the Enveloppe additions. Drawing, c. 1669

complement the architectural grandeur of its spaces and plantings. A high building was needed. On the other hand the preservation of the old château as the eastern side of the new building made this very difficult, particularly since the château was generally approached and seen first from a high point (see Fig. 4). The western or garden side could not appear to rise above the roof of the old château. The solution was a clever one, dating back to the time of the first Enveloppe scheme of 1668 or earlier (Fig. 30). The mansard slate roof of the old château was preserved and slightly altered, while on the garden side an Italian arrangement with columns, pilasters and a roof hidden by a balustrade was introduced. The Italianate articulation allowed for the addition of a full floor above the height of the walls of the old château.

The handsome yellow-white stone façades of the garden front as they now stand (Fig. 35) refine and improve the earlier plan for them. But even these façades were carefully developed from functional needs and as responses to specific architectural problems.

Le Vau's designs for these walls have often been considered to be his masterpiece. However, the triumph lies in his coping ingeniously with problems posed by the preservation of previous buildings. An example is his solution for the elevations of the north and south walls (Fig. 35). The

35. The north and west walls of the Enveloppe palace of Versailles (as revised by Hardouin-Mansart in 1678).
Photo by Atget

difficulty there (clearly an agonizing one if Colbert's written remarks are taken seriously[18]) was that three protruding supportive elements from the 1668 walls remained on each side. If a wall was designed in which these three elements retained a symmetrical relationship, there would not have been enough room for the royal apartments (specifically, for a sufficient number of rooms *en enfilade* for the king). It was eventually decided that the walls had to be extended in spite of the resulting asymmetry. This may be seen in Fig. 35. It was the architect's task to hide this irregularity.

He brilliantly managed this by the three-part vertical articulation of the façade. The top storeys had no projections for their entire length. By a clever use of an Ionic order of pilasters and columns along the middle floor, or *piano nobile*, and by changing from pilasters to full column orders in the areas over the offending projections, a flattened effect was achieved (Fig. 35).

Interestingly, this manoeuvre actually produced one of the most attractive

36. Israel Silvestre: view of the château of Versailles from the north, with the Pool of Clagny in the foreground. Engraving, 1674

and original aspects of the design. It was traditional in similar Italian buildings to decorate the roof balustrades with trophies, vases or other sculptural elements, but at Versailles figures stand above the columns directly in front of the top storey.

Le Vau's treatment of the actual extensions to the east of the 1668 walls was less successful. The top floor at each of the east ends had two gables (see Fig. 36), probably to reflect the position of the chapel originally located at the east end of the queen's apartment on the south side.

37. *Anonymous: the west (terrace) side of the Enveloppe palace of Versailles, with a project for the west parterre*
(M.V. 727). Painting, c. 1670

Le Vau died unexpectedly in October of 1670. Fortunately by then the exterior shell of the Enveloppe had been fully determined. It was up to others to resolve the many problems of the interior.

While no memorandum survives to explain the programme or the full project for the palace and park which emerged during Le Vau's time, a large drawing today in Stockholm provides interesting information about the thinking of Louis's administrators and designers (Fig. 38). Their idea

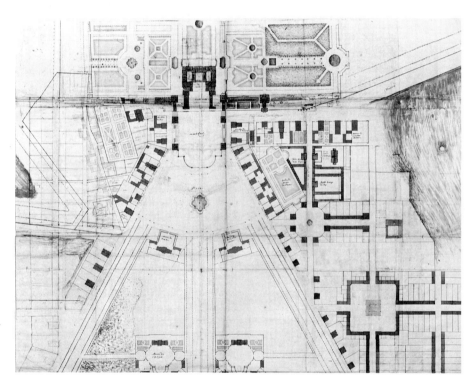

38. Plan of Versailles showing the town, a part of the gardens and the château (T.H.C. 2). Drawing, partly coloured, 1669 or 1670

seems to have been to put the accent on the park and town and to locate the alternative facilities to the suppressed great ceremonial rooms in the park rather than in the château itself. Two spectacular features can clearly be seen in the plan. An enormous opera house was to be constructed as a separate building to the south (to the left of the château in Fig. 38). Far to the north (to the right of the château in Fig. 38), at the end of a group of four reservoirs, a large pavilion for entertainments was planned; it was to be a partial replacement for the ceremonial rooms of Le Vau's aborted palace. This pavilion suggests that the idea was to give permanent form to some of the amenities that had recently been constructed in temporary form in the garden for the *fête* of 1668. It implies that it was the king's intention to continue the country retreat tradition of Versailles of the 1660s, the days of the Enchanted Palace, rather than to build the new royal residence he planned in 1669.

In this context it appears that the interior of the Enveloppe must have been primarily intended to provide living space for the king and his immediate family; in fact, the plans and documents which survive tend to confirm this. On the north side, the King's Great Apartment, his living space, was to occupy most or all of the main upper floor (Premier Étage). The ground

39. South elevation of a project for the former King's Bathroom at Versailles. Drawing, c. 1671

floor below it was destined for a spectacular royal bath (Fig. 39), while the whole *enfilade* of rooms along the north side of the ground floor appears to have eventually been destined for use as reception rooms. Two salons, named after the ancient orders, Doric and Ionic (Fig. 40), and a grand cabinet treated as an octagon were conceived in 1671. All these rooms were referred to on plans as 'the Lower Apartment of His Majesty'. The rest of the royal family was to be housed in nearly equal grandeur behind the south façade of the new palace. The queen was to occupy the whole upstairs floor; the apartments of the king's only brother and his family and those of the little dauphin were to be on the ground floor.

From what is known of the building history of the interior of the Enveloppe it would appear that first priority was given to the magnificent decoration of the Lower Apartment of the King. Two rooms were painted with illusionistic architecture by Colonna, the famous Bolognese specialist in this type of painting, and the Doric, Ionic and Octagonal Salons were encrusted with marble, sculptural reliefs and life-sized statues of figures. The life-sized

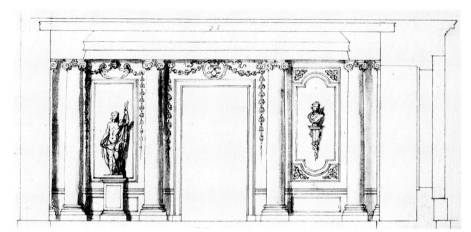

40. *West elevation of a project for the Ionic Salon of the Lower Apartment of the King at Versailles (G.M. 8240). Drawing, inscribed: 'le Roy veu les figures ... 28 mai 1671'*

statues of the Octagonal Salon representing the months were particularly impressive, being made after the designs of Le Brun (Fig. 41).

The surviving plans for the Enveloppe with the terrace raise a number of important problems about the intended functions both of specific areas and of the building as a whole. For example, the Grand Apartments of both the King and the Queen are really without precedent in earlier royal architecture, either in France or in the rest of Europe.[19] The seven or eight major rooms connected to each other for each of the monarchs represent apartments almost twice the normal size. If the Lower Apartment of the King is added to the eight upstairs rooms he would have had the staggering total of thirteen huge rooms for his accommodation alone. The position of the royal chambers is also startling, removed from the stairway by four ante-chambers in the case of the king, and even supplemented with one or more additional private bedrooms further behind in the sequence of rooms. It is hard to believe that all of this represents any ideal functional scheme; some projects of this era seem to be fantasy rather than good architecture.

One project would have changed the area of the terrace and the interior of the old château into a vast central vestibule (see Fig. 111). It was rejected around 1674 in favour of the retention of the terrace and the creation of smaller, informal bedrooms facing directly on to it (Fig. 42). A plan in Stockholm (Fig. 43) gives an excellent idea of the state of the château at that time and of the location of the terrace bedrooms; it contains so many beds in the royal suites that it is impossible to determine who was supposed to sleep where.

In spite of certain well-established details of the history of these new

Tom. 1. Pag. 62.

41. *After Charles Le Brun: a sculpture executed by Le Hongre, now destroyed, representing the month of September for the Octagonal Salon at Versailles. Engraved by Serugue*

42. Cross-section of the
terrace and lower gallery of
the château of Versailles,
view from the south, with a
project for a small bedroom
for the king off the terrace
on the Premier Étage of the
old château. Drawing, 1670s

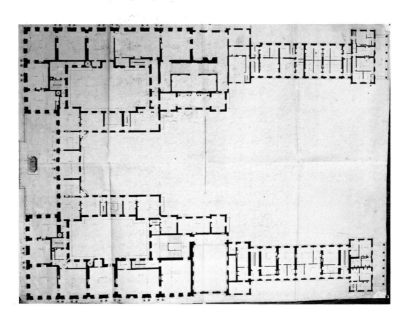

43. Plan of the Premier
Étage of the château of
Versailles (C.C. 74).
Drawing, between 1674
and 1678

apartments, much of the story of what actually happened during the early 1670s remains obscure. Certainly, some important projects must have been undertaken, brought to near completion, then disappeared without a trace. The several versions of the king's stairway to his Grand Apartment is a good example of this. My recent discovery of a project for a gallery at the head of the king's stairway (Fig. 44), for which final payment was made for the alabaster pilasters in 1671, may serve as a case in point. This room must have been designed because the need for a large public area became clear shortly after the plan of 1669 was reformulated; the placement of a gallery at the head of the stairs was useful since it served to keep quite separate the private and more public areas of the king's residence. (In this arrangement Louis's guard room followed the gallery.) But, once built, it must have been evident that the north-facing windows at only one end of the room simply would not provide enough light for so grand a space. Furthermore, the idea of a gallery not aligned with the rest of the apartment certainly was awkward. This project would seem to illustrate the rather hit-and-miss character typical of some of this phase of the planning of Versailles, a phase which was surely the result of the chaotic early history of the building of the Enveloppe.

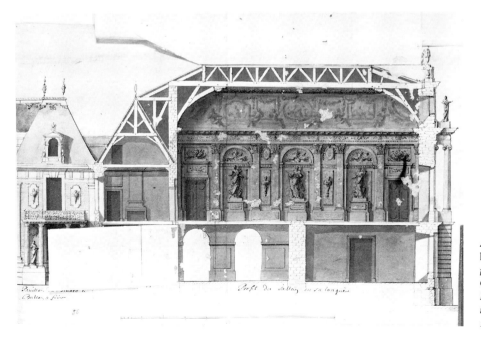

44. Profil du Salon en sa longueur, *cross-section of a project for a gallery for the Grand Apartment of the King at Versailles, showing the western wall. Drawing, 1670 or 1671*

CHAPTER 7

THE PALACE OF
APOLLO

(1670–77)

I t must have been during 1671, when the exterior of the Enveloppe palace was just about complete, that Félibien wrote his famous statement about Versailles. 'Since the sun was the emblem of Louis XIV and poets fuse the sun and Apollo,' he declared, 'everything at Versailles was related to that Greek god.' This was said in a guide of 1674 which was rapidly produced to celebrate the completion of the Enveloppe. Félibien's statement boldly announced one of the principal novelties of the new building, that it had an elaborate programme of images.

Neither Mademoiselle de Scudéry's comments nor those of La Fontaine, both written in 1668, suggest any such programme. The Apollo myth first appeared during the sixties, but it was far from all-pervasive then. The great labyrinth was more symptomatic of the imagery of that earlier era. This large section of the garden appears to have been designed for the amusement and the instruction of Louis's heir, the dauphin. Apollo had no place there. The many animal fountains (Fig. 46) illustrated episodes from Aesop's *Fables*, recently rendered in French by La Fontaine, and the gate was decorated with statues of Aesop and an Amor.

Colbert's new cultural institutions probably explain the adoption of the iconographic programme mentioned by Félibien. The history of the Petite Académie or Académie des Inscriptions which is attached to the first volume of the deliberations of this body contains the following statement: 'All of the projects for the paintings which decorate the apartments of Versailles were made by this organization. The drawings of fountains and the statues were decided upon [*pris et arrestés*] and there was nothing in the [royal] buildings which was not discussed in the Petite Académie.' The very close connection of the Petite Académie with Versailles was fostered by the fact that its secretary was Charles Perrault, who, though now best-known as the author of the fairy tales, worked at Versailles organizing and inspecting both the building and the installation of art works as Colbert's right-hand man.

45 (opposite). François Girardon: Apollo and the Muses, *made for the Grotto of Thetis, now in an eighteenth-century setting designed by Hubert Robert. Marble sculpture, 1666–72*

46. *The Fountain of the Crane and the Swan in the labyrinth of Versailles. Engraving by Le Clerc*

The programme of images made itself felt most prominently on the sculptural decoration of the exterior architecture of the new palace, particularly on the sides facing the garden. The new façades included locations above the columns suitable for over-life-sized allegorical figures. Charles Le Brun was given the job of formulating the allegories and provided highly finished drawings for the sculptors to execute. The subjects of the twelve female figures which were made for the west front suggest the omnipresent character of the sun. The twelve statues represent the twelve months of the year and are associated with the twelve signs of the zodiac which form the path of the sun through the heavens during the year. The months begin at the south end with March, as did the year in ancient times. The coldest months were at the north end where one would expect to find them (Fig. 47).

With the famous *Iconographia* of Cesare Ripa in hand as he designed the figures, Le Brun had it within his power to suggest all kinds of fine points. For example, the sunny south side featured the flowers and fruits of the garden, and the arts, particularly the theatre, were also recalled since an opera house was to be located near this wall (see Fig. 38). The statues on the north wall related to the Grotto of Thetis (then nearby) and thus to the sea and water (quite possibly also a reference to the fountains of the park

47. *Balthazard and Gaspard Marsy: female figures representing January and February, on the central portion of the garden façade of the château. Stone sculptures, 1670–72*

or to the nearby reservoirs which supplied the fountains with water). Agriculture and fishing were also invoked, since food was an appropriate subject in an area of party rooms with kitchens nearby. Félibien says: 'All the figures and ornaments that one sees were certainly not placed by chance, they are related either to the sun or to the particular places where they are placed.'

So far did the search for significant symbolism go that an attempt was made to tie in even the ornaments on the keystones of the arches of the ground floor and some small reliefs of putti over the square windows. The Marsy brothers created some of their masterpieces in the keystones with

48. Attributed to the Marsy brothers: keystone of the eighteenth arch of the ground floor of the garden façade, in the form of an old woman's head. Stone sculpture, 1673 or 1674

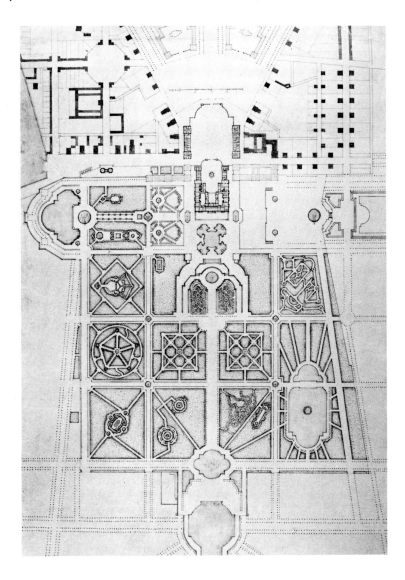

49. Plan of the château, gardens and town of Versailles, detail (Inv. 33014). Drawing, inscribed '1680'

subjects related either to the mythological scheme or to the theme of the passage of time and the ageing of men and women, a reference to the solar time units of days and years (Fig. 48).

The old brick château, still visible on the east side, also received new allegorical sculptures (see Fig. 32).

Infatuation with these allegorical decorations seems to have become so great that just before 1674 the decision was made to carry the symbolism beyond the buildings into the park with a large order for very expensive marble sculptures for the western parterre just below the terrace of the château. Colbert commissioned twenty-eight over-life-sized marble sculptures.

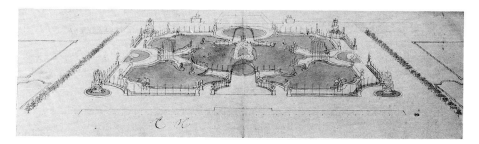

50. Project for a western parterre in front of the garden façade of Versailles, shown as it would have been seen from the terrace (G.M. 8171). Drawing, c. 1673-4

Charles Le Brun also undertook the design of these works. They included a large globe and two types of sculptural groups, four of two or three large figures and twenty-four of only one. The larger groups were all scenes of rapes from classical antiquity inspired by famous sculptures of similar subjects by Gianbologna and Bernini (Persephone by Pluto, Cybele by Saturn, Orithyia by Boreas, Coronis by Neptune). In the context of the parterre they were to represent the four elements (e.g. Neptune as water, Boreas air). The single-figure sculptures, all allegories, were more or less derived from Ripa and were six groups of four statues representing various themes: the seasons (Fig. 51); the elements (repeated from the larger groups); the four times of the day; the four parts of the world; the four poems; and the four humours of men.

Unfortunately the written programme which would explain the relationship of all these subjects to Apollo or to the sun has not survived, but Claude Nivelon, the early biographer of Charles Le Brun, said the programme was intended to suggest 'the union or linkage which composes the universe'. Since it had been established in the seventeenth century that the sun was the centre of the planetary system, and since at the time it was thought that the stars reflected the sun's light and related to the sun as a

51. Charles Le Brun: the Four Seasons, a project for four statues of the Grand Command (G.M. 5956). Drawing, c. 1674

kind of court, a point made by Louis XIV himself, the meaning contained in the programme is reasonably clear.

The solar obsession of these years was expressed not only in the exterior sculpture but also in the interior. Figure sculptures related to the months were the principal decoration of the Octagonal Salon in the King's Lower Apartment (Fig. 41), and the main rooms of the Grand Apartments of both the King and the Queen were given ceilings with planetary motifs.

The idea of using the planets as the theme for these apartments must have sprung easily to mind since there was a very important precedent for it in another famous garden palace, the Palazzo Pitti in Florence. Pietro da Cortona and his assistants had provided a sumptuous ceiling decor of gilt plaster architecture (and sculpture) framing historical pictures and others representing the gods and goddesses after whom the planets were named. These decorations were well-known in France, the style having been employed by Pietro's student Romanelli in Paris. He had produced an approximation of the Pitti decorations in some rooms decorated for Anne of Austria at the Louvre during the 1650s. It may also be relevant that the sixth and final planetary room in Florence was undertaken only in 1663–5, and therefore the decor cannot have been considered out of date in the 1670s.

But what was produced at Versailles, while grandly gilded in the manner of the Pitti and superficially similar in subject matter, was in many ways very different, particularly in the message the pictures were expected to convey. At the Pitti the rooms of the apartments, as at Versailles, were *en enfilade*, or to be visited one after the other. Five of them honoured Venus, Apollo, Jove, Mars and Saturn. Their message was very serious, and the decor was intended to serve as an *exemplum* for the Tuscan rulers.[20] The images suggested the acquisition by the Florentine prince (by means of the gifts of the gods of the virtues) of the qualities of a great ruler. The sequence of the rooms was also of interest. 'In the planetary cycle, bestowal of the virtues of rulership occurs in a sequential order. The sequence is evolutionary in character, for as the prince matures from childhood to youth, he ascends from a land-based Venus to a skyborne Apollo ... At the initiation of the planetary cycle, in the *Sala de Venere* [Venus], the prince is snatched by Minerva [Wisdom] from the pleasures of Vice personified by Venus and presented with an appropriate mentor, Hercules ...' The *Sala de Venere* shows the prince's choice between Virtue and Vice and can serve to illustrate the high moral tone of all of the Florentine rooms.

Before Versailles, Nicholas Mignard and Nicholas Loyr had decorated the bedroom and ante-chamber of the king at the Tuileries palace in Paris with the theme of Apollo. Mignard's four paintings, which surrounded an Apollonian element in the centre, contained 'four important lessons'. His *Punishment of the Cyclopses* illustrated 'the risks taken by those unwise enough to supply arms to the enemies of the king', while *The History of Niobe* represented 'the inevitable disaster which came to those who lacked respect for the sacred personage of a powerful monarch.' Mignard's *Plea of Marsyas* described 'the punishment due to those *gros* and presumptuous people who dared to presume to equal the prince in the art of leading his people', and the final history, *The Example of Midas*, taught 'how much those people render themselves ridiculous either by ignorance or by envy in wishing to make disadvantageous comparisons to the glory of His Majesty.' Loyr's four pictures taught the courtiers their obligations to the crown in a similar manner.[21] The royal painters thus opted for a direct didactic approach far less subtle than the Florentine images.

The striking contrast in the message of the Versailles ceilings to *both* the Pitti and even to the Tuileries ceilings is conveyed in an early guide published under the pseudonym of the Sieur Combes in 1681. About the ceiling of the Venus Salon (Fig. 52) Combes writes:

The painting of the middle of the ceiling is a Venus crowned by the three graces rendering subject to her empire Divinities and Powers; ... the Divinities that she subjects to her law are Mars, who carries a standard, and Vulcan, who carries a hammer and a casque, Bacchus, who wears a wreath of ivy on his head, Jupiter,

with his sceptre and eagle, and Neptune, with his trident. The Powers are four heroes, two from history and two from mythology, shown in the four corners of the ceiling in the form of captives bound with garlands of flowers. Those from history are Titus, who marries a Jewish slave after the destruction of Jerusalem, and Mark Antony and Cleopatra. Those from mythology: Jason and Medea, Theseus and Ariadne . . .

Combes' description goes on to mention such subjects as Nebuchadnezzar building the gardens of Babylon for his wife, who longed for the mountains of her childhood. The moral message at Versailles has almost disappeared.

The Venus Salon was of relatively late date, after 1680. Combes' description of the earlier Versailles room, the Apollo Salon, the central element of the king's apartment, is even less explicit in its message. 'One sees in the picture in the middle of the ceiling Apollo on his chariot pulled by four horses; he is accompanied by the four seasons . . . Near the chariot are magnanimity and magnificence [as female allegories] with France [also a lady] who rests on the cares of the sun, which is the king's emblem [*Heiro-gliphe*]' (Fig. 53). No explanation whatever is given of the four stories from history which are represented above the cornice: Augustus building a port near Messina; Vespasian, who is said by Combes to have built the Coliseum; Coriolanus, who raises the siege against Rome; and the death of Porus, 'King of India'. What is probable here is that all the stories are references to the actions of Louis XIV, such as the rebuilding of the French navy (though astrological connections and the like should not be entirely excluded). But this point was surely not widely understood. Combes was not privy to it, and yet his sources of information, according to his introduction, were no lesser personages than Antoine Coysevox, the sculptor, and Charles de Lafosse, the painter of the central panel of the Apollo room in question.

At Versailles, it was probably the position of the planets and the sequence of the planetary rooms which were of the utmost importance. The bedchamber of the king was predictably to be dedicated to Apollo. A solarcentric message was certainly the principal meaning of the apartments of both the king and the queen. It harmonized well with the kind of programme found in the sculptural decoration of the exterior of the buildings.

The question remains to be answered whether underneath the apparently unsubtle programme of the Versailles ceilings there were hidden some important ideas which escape us today but which might render Versailles more comparable to the Pitti decor than has been suggested above. In 1678 *Mercure galant*, a monthly journal, actually printed a picture and invited readers' explanations, which were published the next month. While explaining why many responses which contained incorrect identifications were

52 (opposite). René Houasse and others: Venus Crowned and other scenes of the loves of princes and mythological scenes. Painted ceiling, before 1681

published, the editor remarked that he would be happy to print wrong answers 'because they are almost always accompanied by some bit of erudition or of history . . .' and he even welcomed the diversity of the responses. In an era when an incorrect identification or interpretation was deemed nearly as valuable as a correct one if it had rhetorical quality, wit and was *à propos*, we must treat all explanations with caution.[22]

The solution to this problem of interpretation is made more difficult still by the facts of the history of the paintings. The payment records indicate that some moving about of the canvases took place. Ceilings were spoken of as in the process of restoration in such a manner as to suggest that the framing elements were importantly changed. Some paintings were even shown completely out of context in Paris at the Salons of the 1670s, before they assumed their final positions. The reordering of pictures in rooms may very well have taken place, particularly since the building was taking shape only haltingly. Under these circumstances a very subtle programme seems hardly likely, and if one existed at the outset it seems to have lost much of its interest during the time taken for the realization of these decorations.

One is tempted to ask whether the Apollo programme at Versailles was really as important as Félibien suggested it was, as many subsequent writers have assumed. Félibien's guide may even have been the expression of the attitude of one group, the painters and sculptors. Félibien was very close to Charles Le Brun.

For Le Brun the death of Le Vau in 1670 held the promise of an increase of influence. Le Brun's situation was certainly aided by the fact that, in 1671, it was primarily work on the interior of Versailles which was needed, a situation ripe for exploitation by an ambitious painter, especially one who got on very well with Louis XIV. Le Brun seems at first to have been extremely successful and in fact to have substantially increased his influence.

By the second half of the 1670s, however, the influence of Le Brun and his colleagues at the Academies of Painting and Sculpture seems to have been in a decline. Possibly it was a matter of political intrigue now unknown, or perhaps Louis XIV somewhat wearied of the proliferation of complicated, erudite mythological programmes made up in his honour. It was inevitable that the King's Buildings Office would assert the equality if not the superiority of architecture and garden design to the figurative arts.

53 (opposite). Charles de Lafosse and others: Apollo in his Chariot and other historical and mythological scenes. Painted ceiling, 1670s

NEW
ATTITUDES

(1678–81)

The Dutch War of the 1670s ended in a victory for Louis XIV. He himself said of it: 'I was resolved to make peace . . . but I wished to conclude it gloriously for me and advantageously for my kingdom. I wished to reimburse myself by the rights of conquest . . . and to console myself thus for the end of a war that I had fought with both pleasure and success.' In the last year of the war Louis had taken the city of Ghent by siege (the Glory) and established definitive possession of the large territory of the Franche-Comté in the east (the Reimbursement). If he had failed to humiliate the Dutch as he had wished, he was at least able in the series of peace treaties signed at Nijmegen to impose his will on the other powers of Europe over certain important issues. Louis's success paved the way for peace in Europe for ten years. Since he believed he was triumphant in Europe he appears to have been ready to move promptly from the projects of a war which had brought profit and glory to his reign to projects of peace which could also add to his renown. Writing to the king during the 1660s Colbert had said: 'Your Majesty knows that with the exception of brilliant military actions nothing speaks so eloquently of the grandeur and cleverness of princes than buildings.' These words were certainly in the king's mind in 1678.

However, the situation at Versailles at that moment was far from brilliant. Important projects were in a state of only partial completion. It seems to have been as much as Colbert could do to provide the king and queen with reasonably comfortable bedrooms.

It must also have been clear that the building under construction no longer met the needs of its owner. The Enveloppe as described by Colbert in 1669 was supposed to house the king and his court for reasonably long sojourns, but Louis's success in forcing his principal nobles to serve him constantly had already created a court too large to fit into the new building. And more space than anticipated was used up by the expanding government bureaucracy; even the king's immediate family began to pose a problem. Many of the children the king had fathered with Madame de Montespan and Mademoiselle de La Vallière were granted princely status (they had been legitimized in 1673). In this context Jules Hardouin-Mansart was able to make himself indispensable to Colbert.

Mansart had understood what was in favour in the mid-1670s, namely, elaborate decorative programmes honouring the king. His first works for Versailles were the pavilions of the Fountain of Fame (Fig. 54). Mansart showed his powers as a designer of ornament in this work, beginning modestly. Later he was able to assert himself.

François d'Orbay, Le Vau's apparent successor, was soon passed over. In 1678 Mansart designed a number of grandiose projects for remodelling both

the old château and the newer Enveloppe. These suggest that he had confidently assumed the position of first architect.

In several projects for Versailles, one or two large new floors were added on top of the existing three (Fig. 55). For the most part Mansart's plans added new space by vertical development, while all that had been done,

54. Israel Silvestre: the Fountain of Fame at Versailles (a bosquet). Engraving, 1682

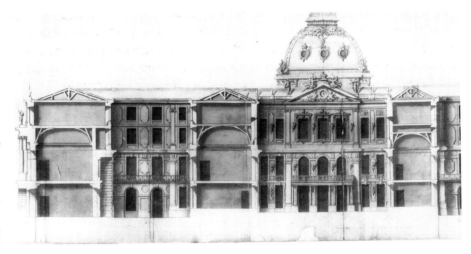

55. Workshop of Mansart: elevation with cross-sections, seen from the east, of a project for the vertical expansion of the palace of Versailles, detail. Coloured drawing, probably 1678

including even the old château of Louis XIII, was to be saved. The elevations of Mansart were certainly made for purposes of discussion; the profusion of alternative designs under flaps on these sheets supports this interpretation.

One pair of drawings proposes alternative solutions for the treatment of the central court and western front of the palace. One sheet appears to be

56. Workshop of Mansart: southern elevation showing the vertical expansion of the northern part of the château of Versailles (with a cross-section of the proposed interior of the central corps de logis, including a great gallery and a high salon). Coloured drawing, probably 1678

the final version of the vertical plan (Fig. 56); the other leaves most of the palace as it was and suggests only the filling in of the terrace on the west

57. Workshop of Mansart: southern elevation of the northern part of the château of Versailles as it stood about 1678, with cross-sections showing the interiors of a great gallery and salon. Coloured drawing, probably 1678

front (Fig. 57). Taken together they show a high degree of imagination in their quite different solutions to the problem of the expansion of the château.

The great roofs, cupolas and even chimneys of some of the plans (e.g. Fig. 55) represent a strong affirmation of the traditional royal architecture of France, perhaps most specifically of the sixteenth-century Tuileries palace renovated only a few years before by Le Vau. Mansart was able to suggest that he was his own man and no slave to the fashionable Italianism. It could hardly have hurt him to show the possibilities of using a national rather than foreign style at a court whose aim was to assert the supremacy of France. But it was also typical of Mansart's tact that he should have also suggested the alternative possibility (Fig. 57), a continuation of what had gone on before. Such an approach vindicated the king's good taste.

It is unfortunate that the surviving elevation of the simplest plan cuts only east-west (Fig. 57). But it must be presumed that north and south wings were conceived at this point. Surviving drawings for a projected detached south wing to be built of brick and stone along the east side of the south parterre suggest that a north–south development rather than vertical building was decided upon as the result of this phase of imaginative thinking.

It was only with the more subtle task of revising this design and of building the great gallery on the site of the terrace, which was later known as the Hall of Mirrors, that Mansart first demonstrated his real genius as an architect. He was able to create great interiors while at the same time preserving and improving the appearance of the exterior walls of the Enveloppe palace. There are enough surviving preliminary studies for the Hall of Mirrors to understand Mansart's creative process.

Mansart had less than a free hand. The acceptance of the project was directly related to the successful completion of a project for the painted ceiling by Le Brun. The surviving written documents are uniquely concerned with Le Brun's programme. According to Nivelon, the crucial point in the history of the gallery came at the famous secret meeting of the king's council when Louis decided to scrap a project representing the deeds of Hercules and to replace them with a representation of the triumph of the king in the Dutch War. The story underscores the fact that for the king the subject matter of the ceiling was more important than the qualities of the rest of the interior design. Mansart was forced at the outset to take what must be considered a supporting role; but eventually he turned the situation to his considerable advantage.

The task which first faced the architect of the gallery was to provide as large a painting surface as possible, while producing a room both light enough to make the reading of the ceiling's message easy and handsome enough in its proportions to provide a worthy frame for a painted programme dedicated to the glory of the monarch. Mansart won Colbert's approval of a plan for both the gallery and a refurbishing of the central room of the old château on 26 September 1678 (Fig. 58). Since nothing less than stupendous would do for so important an enterprise, the decision was made to use the entire area of the terrace and to suppress two large rooms in each of the new Apartments of the King and Queen (see Fig. 43). For so large a room there could be no question of a ceiling only one floor high, and in the first project the use of two entire floors was planned.

This design certainly provided a handsome and worthy architectural space, but it had a serious, even fatal shortcoming: the illumination of the ceiling. A series of small openings just above the architectural frieze at the top of the first storey was the solution proposed by Mansart; but this indirect lighting would never have made the ceiling paintings visible on a normal day. Soon it was back to the drawing boards.

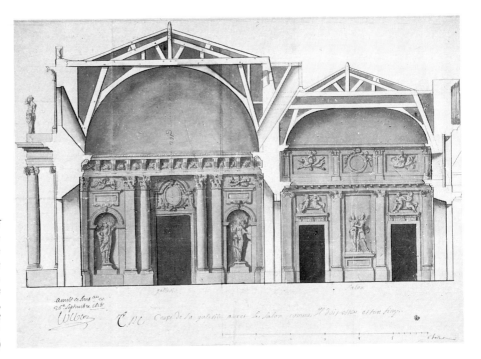

58. Workshop of Mansart: elevation of the north walls of the new gallery and salon of the château of Versailles. Drawing, inscribed as approved for execution, dated 26 September 1678 and signed 'Colbert' (G.M. 8438)

Mansart seems to have perceived at this time that only by devices other than the use of light from above could the ceiling receive the necessary illumination. By the spring of 1679 he decided to lower the ceiling somewhat and came up with an important and famous element of his successful final design: the idea of using mirrors on those walls without windows to increase the light (see Fig. 11). This was a stroke of genius, a happy solution not only in terms of the illumination but also drawing attention to the quality of the architectural design in a spectacular and extravagant way. The price of mirror glass, which at the time had to be imported from Venice, made this a very grand gesture. One other aspect of the design seems to have been cleverly conceived to shift some of the attention from the paintings to the design of the gallery itself. In response to a famous request for a French order by Colbert (of 1671), Mansart provided a new French column capital (order) for the pilasters along the side of his gallery in 1678 (Fig. 59).

The last important element of the final plan developed logically from the ideas behind the use of mirrors for illumination. It was the treatment of the windows themselves. What Mansart did was to open up as much of the west wall as he could to admit light within the constraints of the orders of columns and pilasters on both the interior and exterior wall elements. He

59. Capital of a pilaster using Mansart's 'French order'. Versailles, Hall of Mirrors

60. Workshop of Mansart: various window projects for the Hall of Mirrors of Versailles. Drawing, probably 1678

experimented with various shapes (Fig. 60), eventually choosing one which added to the form of the earlier rectangular windows of the Enveloppe a semicircular top along the lines of an admirable ancient Roman prototype, going back ultimately to the articulation with engaged columns and arches of the exterior of the Coliseum. Mansart's final touch was the suppression of the window sills and the lowering of all of the windows to the floor (making French windows), which helped the illumination of the interior. This fenestration and ordering was then duplicated on the opposite side of the gallery, with the glass replaced by mirrors.

Mansart was even able to turn this ingenious solution for the interior to good effect elsewhere. His second, but equally important interest was the exterior of the Enveloppe palace with the gallery in the place of the terrace. The new window shape served him well there too. Le Vau's articulation of the garden front had not produced an altogether elegant result, the rather low rectangular windows with putti reliefs above them appearing somewhat squat. With his rounded windows (see Fig. 35) Mansart seems to have evolved a more attractive façade which evoked, more than Le Vau had done, the feeling of the great architecture of sixteenth-century Italy. Such a masterpiece as Sansovino's Biblioteca in Venice comes immediately to mind.

The repeated curves of the arches of Mansart's new façade also added a note of grace quite absent earlier, and these windows were also able to solve another functional problem – the poor illumination of the King's Grand Apartment. Mansart cleverly decided to redo all the windows on the north and south façades of the palace to harmonize with the articulation of the gallery front. This brought much-needed extra light to the king's rooms (which faced north).

The serious planning of the painted decoration of the Hall of Mirrors occurred simultaneously with Mansart's architectural work. At first Le Brun had begun in a thoroughly conventional manner, choosing a subject in complete harmony with the mythological programme of the 1670s. The subjects were stories of Apollo and Diana, the sun and the moon. A surviving drawing suggests that the date of the first Apollo decor coincided with the decision by Mansart to use mirrors.[23]

But probably sensing the need to excel in competition with Mansart, Le Brun abandoned the Apollo–Diana project, which was followed rather quickly by another mythological scheme, the Labours of Hercules. The change in programme was made because it was easier to associate the Labours of Hercules with the great actions of Louis's reign. Much work went into this second project, as the splendid drawings for it show (Fig. 61). It was in fact approved, further refined, and then dramatically rejected.

At a long meeting of the council, Nivelon reports, '[His Majesty] found it appropriate and resolved that his history, that of his conquests, should be represented.'

Monsieur Le Brun shut himself away for two days ... and produced there the first drawing [project] of this great work, which is the central image from the centre which forms the nucleus of all the rest; on the basis of this he [Le Brun] was asked to continue the series on these same principles and fine ideas, with the prudent restriction from Monsieur Colbert that there should be nothing there which did not conform with truth, nor anything too irritating to the foreign powers who might figure there.

It is not quite clear how long it took Le Brun to perfect his grand scheme, but there is no reason to think that he rushed to finish it. The painters began the execution only in 1681.[24]

The central scene mentioned above (Fig. 62) shows Louis inspired by

61. *Workshop of Charles Le Brun: Hercules project for the ceiling of the Hall of Mirrors, detail (M.V. 7912).*
Drawing, 1679

Minerva (wisdom); he is dressed as a French king, but wearing elements of Roman armour, and is seated in a grand architectural setting reminiscent of a corner of the Versailles park. He is surrounded by putti and women representing the joys of peace and the achievements, financial, cultural and military, of the reign. The scene was intended to depict Louis's assumption of power in 1661. Behind this scene hover ominous storm clouds, explained by the part of the painting which continues over the ceiling to the other side of the gallery. There three female figures representing the hostile foreign powers sit facing Louis in the midst of arms and mauled captives. They are intended to convey the idea that the peace and prosperity of France are about to be disturbed by foreign plots.

The new scheme simply developed more directly the laudatory idea behind the Hercules programme, and the innovation was far from radical. The depiction of military triumphs on gallery ceilings had precedents, such as the ceiling finished in 1678 by Coli and Gherardi at the Galleria Colonna in Rome, glorifying the exploits of Marcantonio Colonna at the Battle of Lepanto. Louis's celebrated actions during the 1660s had already been woven into tapestries by Le Brun (see Fig. 83). It is largely in the context of the mythological decorations at Versailles that the new programme was a bold stroke. The idea that Versailles was a place of diversion, a country retreat, the palace of Apollo, was suddenly obsolete. In acquiring its gallery Versailles became a monument to the triumphs of the reign.

To discuss in detail the rest of Le Brun's programme would require a book-length study. Perhaps it will suffice here to mention one basic point. The fundamentally new element in the great gallery rests in this: its decoration is only an affirmation of the present reality, considered as the take-off point for Louis's future aspirations.[25] Though the scenes mostly represent events of the Dutch War, the most famous being the order to attack three places in Holland at the same time (1672), the crossing of the Rhine (1672), the capture of Maastricht (1673) and the taking of the city and citadel of Ghent (1678), the message was really to Louis's recent enemies, exhorting them to respect the destiny of so great a power as France under such a king. No one could possibly have missed the message of the supremacy of France and its glorious monarch depicted by Le Brun in *The Crossing of the Rhine* (Fig. 63). The scene, 'the most dramatic in the gallery', shows Louis 'transported as Apollo on a triumphal chariot'. He 'holds up Jupiter's quiver of Thunderbolts; behind him Hercules swings at the old Rhine [god] with his club while at the same time preparations are being made to gather the keys of the cities of Holland for presentation to the king.'[26]

The decorative arrangement of Le Brun's ceiling was effective but can best be described as only moderately up-to-date. Most of the paintings on

62 (opposite). *Charles Le Brun:* The Assumption of Personal Rule by Louis XIV, *central panel of the ceiling. Versailles, Hall of Mirrors*

63. Charles Le Brun: final small study for the Crossing of the Rhine panel of the ceiling of the Hall of Mirrors (G.M. 6507). Drawing, lined for enlargement, 1679?

the ceiling were *quadri reportati*, represented as if they had been painted at eye level and were then put up on the ceiling. They were out of phase with the illusionism current at that moment in Italian ceiling painting. On the other hand, the main scenes occupy only about half the area of the ceiling; the rest shows architecture, decorative nudes and flower garlands and is fully illusionistic. It must have been the intention of Le Brun, a serious history painter, to keep as separate as possible the representations of history and the lesser genre of decoration (Fig. 64). Le Brun's general model was clearly the great ceiling planned but not executed by Giovanni Lanfranco for the gallery of the Benediction Loggia at St Peter's during the second

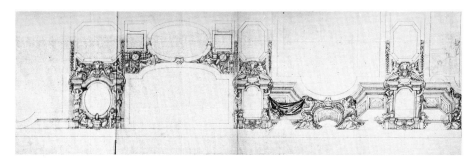

64. Workshop of Charles Le Brun: study for the illusionistic architecture of the ceiling of the Hall of Mirrors (G.M. 5803). Drawing, 1679

65. Reconstruction of Giovanni Lanfranco's project for the ceiling of the gallery of the Benediction Loggia of St Peter's Basilica, Rome. From the engravings of Piero Santi Bartoli published about 1663

decade of the century (Fig. 65). Some of Lanfranco's drawings had been published in 1663. In any event Le Brun's design fitted perfectly with Mansart's architecture, which in its broad lines, as it turned out, was not very different from the gallery at St Peter's.

The great success of the gallery resulted in the decision to include in its grand decorative scheme two further rooms which then occupied, with the gallery, the whole of the western side of the palace. These were then dedicated to the themes of war (Fig. 66) and peace, and their ceilings, also by Le Brun, were a kind of reprise in miniature of the gallery itself. Thus Mansart had created a suite which looked out on the three principal axes

66. Jules Hardouin-Mansart and Charles Le Brun: the Salon of War, with the plaster relief by Antoine Coysevox,
Louis XIV on Horseback Trampling on his Enemies and Crowned by Glory

of Le Nôtre's great park. Being raised a floor above, the gallery enjoyed perhaps the most impressive views of Le Nôtre's creation. Blondel, one of the earliest and most enthusiastic architectural critics to write of the Hall of Mirrors, was particularly impressed by the relationship between the great new apartments and the park, which brings to the visitor

the most beautiful scene that one could possibly imagine by the view of the playing fountains and the gardens of this palace, terminating with the Grand Canal ... From this same area ... there is another view which makes visible the greater part of the full extent of the Versailles gardens from the furthest extent of the Swiss pool [*Pièce d'eau Suisse*, south] to the Pyramid fountain, a charming feature which enhances the beauty of this gallery and contributes more than a little to making it the most beautiful spot in the world ...[27]

The second important manifestation of the linking of the creative forces of Mansart and Le Brun at this time was in the decor for the unfinished

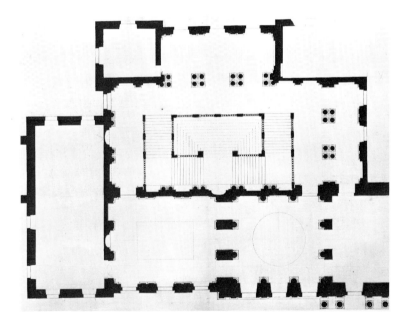

67. Ground plan of a project for the stairway to the Grand Apartment of the King at Versailles and for the rooms of the apartment opening on to it (C.C. 136). Drawing, probably before 1676

great stairway leading to the Grand Apartment (Fig. 67; see also Fig. 7). After many delays, the area seems to have been ready to receive its painted decoration in 1678, the ornamental architectural works apparently being undertaken in the spring. The programmatic painting of the stairwell must have come shortly afterwards, contemporary with the decision to build the Hall of Mirrors, but before the gallery's painted decoration was fully worked out.

All the paintings and sculptures of the area below the ceiling of the stairway relate either to the function of the stairway or to the victories of the king. Louis's bust by Warin, rather than an Apollo or Hercules, was indeed the central element, placed as it was against an elaborate panel of trophies and other royal symbols in the centre of the principal wall. The decorations painted between pilasters on the level of the Grand Apartment were the most striking. On feigned tapestries were represented four important events of the Dutch War from the year 1677, while four other illusionistic paintings, two on each of the two long walls, showed figures from the four parts of the world gazing down on visitors (Fig. 68). These figures were the origin of a new name for the stairway, subsequently called the Stairway of the Ambassadors, since they were clearly based upon the well-

68. Charles Le Brun: The Different Nations of America, *study for the painting for the Stairway of the Ambassadors at Versailles (G.M. 5749). Drawing, c. 1678*

known paintings made earlier in the century for the Room of the Ambassadors in the papal Quirinal Palace in Rome. The older mentality of the Grand Apartment's mythological imagery survived only in the decoration of the ceiling by Le Brun, where Mythology, an allegorical figure, and the Muses wove a complicated account of the feats of the king's reign.

The new parts of the palace forced Mansart to develop a substantial number of important projects for both the old château and the new palace. The king eventually abandoned his Great Apartment and turned these rooms into the principal area for receptions and entertainment. An enormous suite of state rooms then wrapped all around the north and west sides of the Enveloppe.

The most impressive public ritual of the king's daily life when he was in residence unfolded in this area of the palace. In 1681 the chapel of the château was moved from the queen's apartment, where it had been since 1670, to the east end of the Grand Apartment of the King (see Fig. 103). Since Louis XIV was lodged and worked in quarters near the centre of the old château, his progress to his daily devotions moved through the Hall of Mirrors, the Salon of War, and the full length of the Grand Apartment.

The new chapel (Fig. 69), which was considered temporary but was in use for nearly thirty years, was rapidly built to the north-east of the château between the Enveloppe palace and the Grotto of Thetis. The king heard mass there from an upstairs tribune, directly joined to the Grand Apartment. (He descended to the ground floor only for special ceremonies or when mass was said by a cardinal.)

The king needed an alternative lodging for himself. Eventually he decided to make use of most of the area of the old château, the eight rooms which wrapped around the west end of the Cour de Marbre. A stairway in the old south wing of Louis XIII's château had been enlarged to provide access to the Queen's Grand Apartment (see p. 28). In 1681 two ante-chambers for the king were built beyond this on the south side of the court of the old château. They were followed by another ante-chamber and by his bedroom (Fig. 70). Beyond the bedroom was the grandest room of the king's suite, the high new salon at the precise centre of the court of the old château. On the side away from the court (west) the salon opened directly by three doors on to the centre of the Hall of Mirrors (see Fig. 58), while a council chamber and several other more private rooms were reached through the north wall of the salon. (They were also within the old château.) Payments indicate that the bedroom and the salon were finished in time for use by the king in 1683.

For the most part the Grand Apartment of the Queen remained as it was, and she did, in fact, sleep in her bedroom in the great *enfilade* of rooms

CEREMONIE

De la prestation de Serment de fidelité entre les mains du Roy, dans la Chapelle de Versailles, par M.' le Marquis de Dangeau, accusé de la grande Maîtrise de l'Ordre de Nôtre Dame du Mont Carmel, et de S.' Lazare le 18 Decembre 1695.

En presence de Monseigneur le Dauphin, de Monseigneur le Duc de Bourgogne qui étoit dans la tribune, de M.' le Prince et de M.' le Cardinal de Furstemberg, en rochet et en Camail.

Mons.' le Marquis de Dangeau étoit accompagné des S.'' de Rumont, de Bragelonne, Denonville, de Montagnac, de Montaure, de Collins, de Guenegaud, de Tillecour, de Montalets, de Sauleux de Geneüillac, et de la Barre, Anciens Chevaliers et Officiers de l'Ordre.

69. The Oath of Fidelity to the King in the Versailles Chapel by the Marquis of Dangeau on 18 December 1695. *Engraving after the painting by Pezey*

with southern exposures as it had been planned in 1669. But even in her quarters a few changes were made.

Dining rooms were not yet a part of royal palaces in France; the custom was that the kings and queens generally ate in the ante-chambers of their apartments. The main room for dining at Versailles became the largest of the queen's suite, since although the king ate supper in his own ante-chamber, more often than not alone, the Grand Couvert, or midday meal with the queen, took place in her apartment. New royal kitchens were built in a pavilion added to the south side of the palace reasonably close by. The decoration of this salon of the Grand Couvert was originally planned to honour the planet Mars, since its first function was a guards' room. This decoration survived unchanged despite the new function the area came to serve. It differed from the king's Salon of Mars only in that heroic women, mostly queens, appeared instead of great rulers below the god in the heavens.

70. *Elevation of the western wall of the bedroom of the king and of the second ante-chamber (des Bassans). Drawing, 1679–83*

Another vestibule (Fig. 71) further to the east was rechristened the Queen's Guards' Room. Its walls had been splendidly invested with marble, but the painting of the ceiling and other details had not been completed. This was done about 1680, and Félibien lauded the originality of the ceiling, singling out for mention in particular the treatment of the corners. There, in a new vein anticipated only by some aspects of the Stairway of the Ambassadors, mythological figures were replaced by illusionistic representations of contemporary figures in court dress.

Innovation was only one part of the decor of this room, however. Extremely conventional canvases (one on the theme of Jupiter) by Noël Coypel were set into the ceilings and walls. They were originally intended for the decor of the King's Grand Apartment. When not needed there, Coypel's paintings were re-used, either out of expediency or out of respect for the artist. In spite of this curious final mixture of elements, the room is one of the richest interiors of a sumptuous era.

The Queen's Stairway, from which the new guards' room was entered, was magnificently decorated at the time the decor of the guards' room was being completed. Dated drawings of 1680 survive. Though somewhat altered in 1702, the stairway still stands as one of the major achievements of an exceptionally productive era (p. 28).

The years around 1679 and 1680 saw still more fine, richly decorated interiors. Some of this work was quite conventional, for example the

71. *The west and north walls of the Queen's Guards' Room. c. 1680. Versailles,*
Grand Apartment of the Queen

72. *The south and east walls of the Salon of Venus. c. 1681. Versailles,*
Grand Apartment of the King

73. Antoine Houasse:
north-east corner of the
ceiling. Painting, c. 1681.
Versailles, Salon
d'Abondance

decoration of the Salons of Diana and Venus (Fig. 72) in the King's Grand
Apartment. The innovative spirit of the first era of Mansart, however, was
strikingly evident in the decor of the small Salon d'Abondance, the room
which was built to join the Grand Apartment of the King to the new
'temporary' chapel. Even the name suggests a change of approach. The
planetary programme was abandoned. The new room spoke more directly
of the achievements of the king. A number of precious objects from the
royal collection of *objets d'art* were shown. Houasse's painted ceiling was
also unusual at Versailles, abandoning the heavy gold Cortonesque plaster
sculptures and frames used in the adjoining rooms for the illusion of a vast
opening to the sky (Fig. 73).

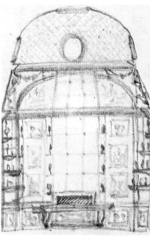

74. *Doorway of the former Cabinet des Curiosités. Marble with painted decorations, c. 1681–2. Versailles, Salon d'Abondance*

75. *Nicodemus Tessin the younger: elevation of the former Cabinet des Curiosités of Versailles (T.H.C. 1315). Drawing, 1687*

The most important architectural feature of the Abundance Salon is the doorway formerly leading to the Cabinet des Curiosités (Fig. 74). Mansart's door represents something of a grand architectural gesture. Its frame actually breaks through the line of the cornice, penetrating the area of the painted ceiling. This had occurred nowhere before at Versailles. The doorway also has a new grace, and there is an inventiveness in the shape that is more reminiscent of Borromini's Rome than of seventeenth-century France; at Versailles this is innovation in the best sense, looking already inevitable, almost classic. Mansart's message in the Salon d'Abondance is the assertion of the primacy of architecture over the painted decoration. The era of Le Brun was coming rapidly to an end.

JOURS
D'APPARTEMENT

(1682–3)

The rebuilding of Versailles around the new gallery proceeded quickly but was such a substantial undertaking that the court absented itself for some time. In the spring of 1682 Louis made it clear that he would like to return as soon as possible and in a different manner from before. By 1680 it had been widely suspected that the king had decided to abandon his capital, Paris, and to establish his residence at Versailles. With the gallery and the many other changes, he was to be better housed at Versailles than he would have been either in the Louvre or at the Tuileries palace. Apart from the political reasons for the move, Louis loved living in the country.

Work on the new Louvre came to a halt: its roof was not completed until the late eighteenth century. In May 1682 the *Gazette de France* reported: 'On the sixth of this month the court left Saint Cloud [the home of Louis's brother] to go to Versailles, where Madame the dauphine was carried in a sedan chair because of her pregnancy, which was very advanced ...' Eventually a male heir was born at the château. This was certainly deliberate, an affirmation of a new status for Versailles.

An anecdote about the rejoicing after the birth gives a sense of the condition of the palace during the summer of 1682: it tells of people pulling up the parquet of unfinished rooms to build bonfires. The scaffolding of the Hall of Mirrors was used for the same purpose. However, by November or December things were more settled, and Louis appears to have decided to present his new residence to the world. Since only a third of the Hall of Mirrors and the Salon of War had been completed, it was the suite of state rooms of the Grand Apartment on the north side of the Enveloppe which was unveiled. In a calculated understatement it was called simply The Apartment.

Colbert made sure that admiring reports were widely circulated. The author of the famous *Description de Versailles* of 1668–9, Mademoiselle de Scudéry, was encouraged to produce an updated sequel, which she did at the end of 1682. The tone of her writing is so enthusiastic that it is clear that the spectacle of the Grand Apartment was overwhelming. She should be allowed to speak for herself:

... And moreover I can assure you, without exaggerating, that you have never seen anything comparable to that which is incorporated in the new word *Appartement*; ... but I predict that whether the Academy [which writes the Dictionary] wishes it or not, it will be as immortal as the glory of *Louis Quatorze* ... never has any word in any language, without exception, signified so great a number of beautiful things ...

[Letter to Philémon in Denmark]

Most contemporaries learned about the Apartment from the December 1682 number of the *Mercure galant* where a long article appeared describing in considerable detail both the entertainments and food and also the appearance of the Apartment at the time. The article was carefully prepared, the writer even describing in some detail the subjects of the painted decorations of the ceilings, enumerating the principal furnishings and commenting on the colour scheme of the hangings and embroideries. This description is unique among those that have come down to us.

The visitor was expected to arrive at the Apartment from the Hall of Mirrors. Since the gallery was only partly completed and its eventual grandeur was suggested only by a perspective rendering on the wall which closed off the area occupied by the painters, the account tactfully began with the Salon of War.

The Salon of War is well preserved today (see Fig. 66), and its architectural and painted decor closely resembles what was seen in 1682. In fact, at the time of the article in the *Mercure*, the plaster relief by Coysevox of Louis on horseback, which is still in place, had just been installed. What are missing today are eight great candle-stands of solid silver which carried candelabra two feet high. The *Mercure* also mentions that each candlestand was accompanied by a pair of vases of the same height and that these groups fitted the spaces between windows and doors. In the corners stood silver vases on bases of gold and blue. A large silver chandelier with eight branches hung from the centre of the ceiling, and below it in the middle of the floor was a silver brazier (Fig. 76).

The first room of the Apartment opened out from the right-hand wall. It was the Salon of Apollo (the former chamber of the king), which in its reincarnation was acting as throne room. The account speaks first of the colour scheme, which was apparently established primarily by the wall coverings above the dado. These were in crimson 'enriched' by thick embroidery in gold. (Bourdelot was specific[28]; the velvet tapestry was decorated with gold embroideries in the form of pilasters.) A table, the guéridons, and

76. Baudoin Yvart: a
brasero or incense burner
on its stand (M.V. 7057).
Study for a Gobelins
tapestry of the series Les
Maisons du Roi. Painting,
c. 1673

77 (opposite). Jean Bérain:
the Hall of Mirrors
furnished and with the
addition of many silver
pieces from the Salon of
Apollo (throne room) on
the occasion of the embassy
from Siam. Engraving, 1686

the ornaments on the fireplace were solid silver. The room was dominated by the throne dais, covered by a remarkable Persian carpet with a gold background. At its centre stood 'A silver throne, eight feet high', which was as much a work of silver sculpture as a piece of furniture. 'Four children carrying baskets of flowers appeared to support the seat and the back, which were decorated with crimson velvet with in relief a bell-shaped ornament in gold. On top in the middle of the back stands Apollo ... Representations of Justice and Force are on either side of him reclining on the curved edge.' The throne and certain other elements of the throne room are best known to us today from an engraving made some years later of the Hall of Mirrors; it shows certain elements of the dais set up temporarily for the reception of the ambassadors of Siam (Fig. 77).

To return to the Salon of Apollo, 'The canopy over the throne is of the same material as the [wall] tapestry. On either side of the throne on the dais [there are] two silver stools also with velvet pillows. On the two corners of the dais there are candelabra eight feet high. All four corners of the room contained silver candle-stands topped with candelabra.' Hanging on the wall tapestry and above the doors, richly framed, were paintings by Rubens, van Dyck, Domenichino (*David*, still at Versailles), and a lovely set of the Labours of Hercules by Guido Reni (now in the Louvre). The floral decorations, such as baskets of cut flowers and potted bushes with scented flowers, are not mentioned but were surely present.

'This room is destined for music and for dancing', says the article in the *Mercure*; and Bourdelot adds some details about the party. Louis did not sit on the throne; three cushions were placed on the edge of the dais and he sat there informally, chatting and watching the dancing and the ladies. The dauphine particularly occupied him, and now, delivered of her son, she was the pre-eminent dancer, Louis himself having stopped more than a decade earlier.

From the throne room the Salon of Mercury was entered. This held a state bed, and, though the room lacked the sensational element of the silver throne, it was no less brilliant. Its pictures, including several by Titian, were first-rate. The wall-covering was similar to that in the throne room; it was crimson at the time, but, as in the throne room, was often changed to green for the summer months. This salon contained a large number of carefully matched elements, such as armchairs, stools and a fire-screen, including the embroidery of the bed, but most striking must have been the solid silver balustrade, two-and-a-half feet high, closing off the bed alcove. Eight silver candelabra stood on the balustrade, and behind it there was beautiful marquetry (inlaid flooring). Another striking element must have been the five-foot-high pair of incense burners which stood in the corners by the bed on solid silver stands. Many other silver objects were included among the

furnishings – from a brazier to an impressive group of ornaments on the
fireplace. Above there was a great silver chandelier with six arms, each one
of which held three candles. (This is often identified as one shown in a
drawing (Fig. 78).) 'Between the windows above a great table one sees a
mirror nine feet high. [On the frame, figures of] Abundance and Magnificence hold the sides of the royal mantle which forms the edge ...' The table
beneath the mirror (see Fig. 79) carried a sensational load of silver – from
baskets to four candelabra; and on either side of the table were the inevitable candle-stands with their branches of candles (compare Fig. 80). In the
middle of the room were three gaming tables exclusively for the royal
family, one pentagonal, one square and one triangular.

*78. A chandelier
representing Fame, similar
to one described by Tessin
as in the Grand Apartment
of the King at Versailles
(C.C. 1549). Drawing,
probably after a Le Brun
design and possibly by
Claude Ballin, before 1678*

*79. After Charles Le Brun:
designs for large console
tables; one is similar to one
of the silver tables shown in
an engraving of the Hall of
Mirrors (C.C. 2389).
Drawing*

The account in *Mercure galant* continues with the rooms where the king
often mixed with the court. It is, perhaps, important to mention, even in a
brief account of these rooms as described, that the Salon of Diana, the
billiard room, contained important works of sculpture, particularly Roman

80. *Daniel Marot: furniture for an area between two windows of a room*
at Het Loo, Apeldoorn. Drawing, dated 1701

81. *Gian Lorenzo Bernini: bust of Louis XIV. Marble sculpture, 1665.*
Versailles, Salon of Diana (see Fig. 9)

busts and some more contemporary works. Bernini's bust of Louis XIV, done during his visit in 1665 was there (Fig. 81).

As Mademoiselle de Scudéry remarked, the Apartment at Versailles was most of all a beautiful place, of the most exquisite refinement. Two elements determined its character: the glorious art collections of the French crown and the products of the new or recently renovated royal manufactories.

The augmentation of the royal collections by the addition of Cardinal Mazarin's made Louis the owner of one of the greatest art collections of Europe. These works were traditionally kept in the châteaux belonging to the king, but before the Apartment it was not traditional to cover walls with masterpieces of painting in abundance. The decision to do so represented an important advance on earlier ideas. By including masterpieces by the very greatest artists as part of the decor, Louis was imitating the great collectors of Italy, such as the Medici, or his father-in-law, Philip IV of Spain. However, the message of this use of art in the context of the refined ideas of French interior design seems to have also been part of a decision to upgrade interior decoration to the level of high art. Once the idea had been established of a room as an integration of various elements into an imposing overall scheme, the addition of high art represented a challenge to the designers to produce furnishings of a calibre worthy of the best objects to be found in the room.

Such ambitions were scarcely new to the king, and he had already paved the way for what happened in the Apartment by appointing Charles Le Brun head of the Gobelins manufactory. The artistic sensibility of this famous painter was clearly enlisted to upgrade the design level of the decorative objects produced there. Tapestries, furniture and massive silver and other metal objects were made, some from Le Brun's own drawings (Fig. 79).

During the 1660s and 1670s a chief ambition of the Gobelins seems to have been the mastery of the technical skills necessary for the production of great works of art. Important foreigners were often highly influential, for example the Italian, Domenico Cucci, who may be said to have established in France the very highest standards of Italy and Flanders in production of luxury furniture.

The great pair of cabinets attributed to Cucci, today at Alnwick Castle, made for Louis in 1681–3 (Fig. 82), gives an excellent idea of what the Gobelins could do at the time of the creation of the Apartment. The lavish combination of rich materials – rare woods, gilt metal, insets of stone, and elaborate stone mosaic panels – and the scale of the work together produced a stunning piece of architectural furniture. Cucci was 'more than anyone else responsible for introducing the note of Italianate richness in the splendid rooms of Versailles, thus establishing a new concept of regal magnificence . . .'[29]

82. *Attributed to Domenico Cucci: a large wall cabinet, said to have been made for the Small Apartment of the King at Versailles. Ebony, gilded metal and wood, with stone and intarsia decorations, 1681–3*

Cucci appears as the dark-complexioned man pointing to a cabinet on Le Brun's famous tapestry (also made at the Gobelins), showing Louis's visit to the manufactory in 1663 (Fig. 83). Along with the Cucci cabinet on the upper right in the tapestry are other examples of furniture, silver and carpets which suggest the rich decor which was assembled in the Apartment, and it is possible that a few of the pieces shown on the tapestry became a part of that decor. Especially likely candidates are the two enormous pitchers of

83. *After Charles Le Brun:* Louis XIV's Visit to the Gobelins. *Tapestry, c. 1729, the sixth series*

84. *Anonymous: solid silver furniture in a throne room (at Versailles?). Drawing, c. 1603*

sculpted silver which appear in the centre of the composition. In 1687 Nicodemus Tessin, visiting Versailles, counted 167 items of solid silver furniture in the state apartments, of which seventy-six were in the Hall of Mirrors, leaving ninety-one mostly for the Apartment. A single drawing survives which gives some kind of an impression of this furniture in place in a room similar to those at Versailles (Fig. 84).

A very sharp distinction was drawn between permanent and movable or, better, removable furnishings. The Grand Apartment was literally transformed by the addition of chairs, tabourets (upholstered stools) and tables during the two or three evenings each week when receptions took place.

A portrait of Madame de Montespan reclining on a day bed (Fig. 85) gives us perhaps the most vivid surviving impression of a grand interior in the tradition of Versailles, although the work was painted about a decade before the Apartment was conceived. Behind Louis's mistress is a view of one of the gallery rooms designed by Hardouin-Mansart at Clagny. The interior is notable both for its vastness and the relative sparsity of its furnishings. The centre of the hall, uncarpeted, is empty with the exception of two elaborately wrought metal objects – clearly braziers, put into the room for heating in the cold months of the year. One of these is accompanied by two small clipped trees in pots, perhaps scented bushes such as orange or jasmine, of which Louis was very fond.

The decoration of one windowed wall can be clearly seen. A dado about four feet high extends the length of the wall, even under the windows. The rest of the furnishings are lined up along this; the principal pieces of furniture occupy the three areas of the wall not pierced by windows. In the centre is, rather predictably, the combination of a table with a massively framed mirror above. On either side of it are large cabinets with bottom stands rather like sculptured tables and large rectangular chests above. The chests are topped with lavish displays of vessels and plates, most likely a mixture of metal objects, ceramics and porcelain. Along the wall are a number of tabourets. An upholstered bench may be discernible along what can be seen of the other back wall. Thus most furnishings are rigidly placed against the walls, with no groupings of tables or chairs in the middle of the room.

The somewhat casual positioning of the luxurious day bed of the Marquise, shown as if on a landing above the hall, is particularly interesting. It implies that such comfortable furnishings, even so large an object as a bed, were more of a temporary intrusion into the setting than a real part of the decorative scheme.

Certain areas of the Versailles Apartment were probably very similar to what is shown at Clagny. The spaciousness of the Clagny gallery was

eventually overwhelmingly achieved in the decor of the Hall of Mirrors. But Versailles was very different, and deliberately so. The rich textiles, the quantity of sumptuous pieces of furniture, the great art – these elements worked together to create an effect which excited even a public accustomed to lavish displays. The *Garde Meuble* and the craftsmen of the royal manufactories managed to create in the decoration of the Apartment precisely the kind of spectacular event appropriate to the opening of an important new phase in the history of the château. The inauguration of the permanent residence of Louis XIV was thus a major event in the history of the decorative arts in France.

85 (opposite). Anonymous:
Madame de Montespan
reclining on a day bed
above a gallery at Clagny.
Painting, 1670s?

COLBERT
AND LOUVOIS

The acclaim which followed the unveiling of the state apartments was not sufficient to allow Colbert to rest on his laurels. He had two problems. The first was personal: his son proved a great disappointment in an important position carved out for him in the superintendency. Despite endless parental admonitions, he was lazy and careless; and since his job was to supervise the completion of important projects, all of which ran late, owing in substantial part to his negligence, the superintendent soon came to feel the anger of the king. However, the basic problem of 1683 might be termed the over-extension of the superintendency. The royal decision to inhabit Versailles produced projects for several enormous new buildings. There

86. Workshop of Mansart: elevation of one side of the Grand Commun of Versailles (T.H.C. 2423). Drawing, c. 1679

were also to be major changes in the gardens and the complete refurbishing of the king's private apartment mentioned above. Deadlines passed and inconveniences occurred so frequently that there was soon talk of Colbert's fall from favour.

In order to catch the flavour of things at Versailles in 1683 it is necessary to enumerate and comment briefly on several of the major projects which were under way. A building half the size of the palace of the Enveloppe, the Grand Commun (Fig. 86), rose to the south-west of the château to house and feed just a few hundred of the members of the king's and queen's households. This building, which still stands, can be clearly seen just to the left of the lower court of the château on the bird's-eye view of Liévin Cruyl of about 1683/4 (Fig. 87). Though in most respects simple and utilitarian, it remains an imposing building because of its height, the vast width of its exterior walls and the size of its inner court, and a refined if somewhat understated decor on the exterior.

Perhaps the best indication of the grandeur of these undertakings is the design of the great stables built on the far side of the great palace square. The king handed over to the queen all of his stables built during the 1670s in the town of Versailles. Then he built two new ones for himself; one was

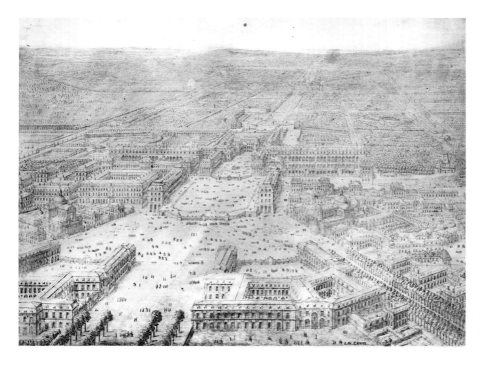

87. *Liévin Cruyl: bird's-eye view of Versailles from the east, with various projects added. Drawing, 1683/4*

for horses for the chase and the other for his coaches and transport. Although these were called the Grande and Petite Écuries they were hardly distinguishable in size, and each was able to house several thousand horses and much of the personnel needed to keep them. An appropriate adjective for these stables might be 'gargantuan'. An idea of their size is given by the Cruyl bird's-eye view (Fig. 87), where they occupy almost the entire foreground, flanking either side of the broad Avenue de Paris, appearing almost to rival the château itself in size.

The architectural design of the stables was outstanding from both the functional and the aesthetic point of view (Fig. 88). Though somewhat in the classical spirit of harmonious proportions and full of references to Italian and ancient architecture, they have a character very much their own that is more than a little French. The two buildings brought a new sense of harmony and grandeur to the approach to the château.

The whole eastern elevation of the château itself was also in the process of changing. The greatest part of the work, which consisted of rebuilding most of the walls of the Cour de Marbre and the joining of four small pavilions to form the two large Wings of the Ministries flanking the forecourt of the château, was nearly complete in 1683.

The palace was also in the process of growing laterally, and a vast south wing, designed especially to house close relatives of the king, was nearing completion (Fig. 89). Its size was colossal. The principal western façade of the wing (overlooking the gardens), while imitating in a general way the appearance of the west façade of the Enveloppe palace after the Hall of Mirrors had been added, was about half as wide again. On the interior it was a very lavish affair. On the Premier Étage, at the point where the wing joined the rest of the château, a small theatre, or Salle de Comédie, was built. Next to it was the large Stairway of the Princes. (This came to serve as a kind of marketplace within the château for the courtiers.) Several of the main apartments of the new wing were hardly inferior in the quality of their design and furnishing to what was being provided in the private apartments of the king himself. The most famous were those created for the dauphin and his wife and those of the Prince and Princess de Conti.

Great works were under way in the area of the garden under the windows of the new south wing. By the end of 1681 there were preparations for the construction of a new Orangery twice the width of the old one by Le Vau. In 1683 the vast excavation of this hillside was nearing completion, and the levelling of the ground for the large *Parterre du Midi* and the two parterres below (which extended out in front of the new Orangery) was under way.

In October 1683 Colbert died suddenly. The Venetian ambassador, Foscarini, stated at the time that his disgrace was near. Louis compared the expenses of Versailles unfavourably with the cost of fortifications erected at the frontier, to Colbert's great distress; Charles Perrault directly attributed his death to this confrontation. The specific circumstances of Colbert's death seem to have caused the surprising rise of his rival Louvois, minister of the army, as a candidate for Colbert's superintendency of the king's buildings.

In spite of his success with fortifications, Louvois was inexperienced and was something of a self-proclaimed philistine in matters relating to the arts.

88 (opposite). Jean-Baptiste Martin: view from the Cour de Marbre of the château of Versailles, across the Cour d'Armes to the Grande and Petite Écuries (stables), with the Avenue de Paris in the background (M.V. 748). Painting, after 1700

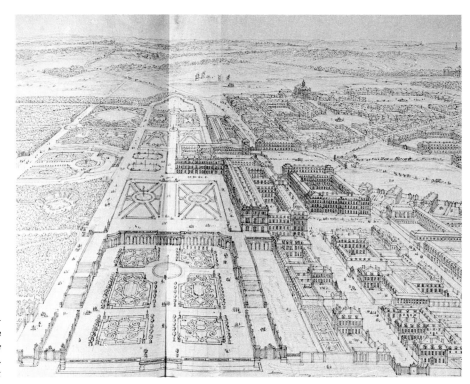

89. Israel Silvestre: bird's-eye view of Versailles seen from the direction of the Satory hill (south) (Inv. 33055). Drawing, 1683–91

A passage in a letter written in 1682 has become notorious: 'Since I am not at all knowledgeable, by which I mean that I do not know anything at all about paintings or statues, I do not want statues which will be costly because of their antiquity; I prefer a pretty copy of highly polished marble to an antique with a broken nose or arm.' Louvois's promotion must have been quite a shock to those at the King's Buildings Office. Colbert had always fancied himself a man of taste, as his remarks on architectural projects make quite clear, and his judgement matured with experience over the years.

Nonetheless, Louis's choice of Louvois appears to have been quickly vindicated. The tone of the memos from the superintendent to the king changed almost at once. Instead of the explanations for delays and the enumeration of problems to which the king had somewhat impatiently become accustomed, suddenly there were lists of things finished and indications of when it was expected that different projects still under way would be completed. Louis was fully informed of exactly what to expect each time he returned to Versailles, and only rarely was he misinformed. Projects which had dragged on for months or years were rapidly completed, and within a year Louis was finally comfortably settled into his private apartments.

In seeking the position of superintendent Louvois certainly knew that he was taking some risks. He was moved to do so by the deep personal involvement of the king in architectural affairs. It was vital to Louvois's overall position in the government that no new personage should emerge with status equivalent to Colbert's.

It is wrong, however, to insist that Louvois had no basis beyond his administrative abilities on which to build a successful administration of the arts. First, there was the substantial legacy of talent left by Colbert at the superintendency, and, second, Louvois was not without interests and friends. His relationship with the celebrated painter Pierre Mignard was certainly one which held promise.

Since Louvois was an enormously ambitious man, it is reasonable to assume that it was his intention sooner or later to assert some personal impact at the superintendency; however, he also knew the king and understood that continuity of policy was a fundamental goal of Louis XIV, who would have felt his prestige compromised by too visible a change of style resulting from the death of one of his ministers. Louvois seems to have begun his administration of the King's Buildings Office and the arts with a policy which operated on two levels simultaneously. On the one hand he rushed the completion of projects initiated by Colbert, so that he clearly demonstrated his remarkable ability to get things done in record time. But he also sought opportunities to initiate impressive new projects, though he was sorely pressed to find areas upon which to make his mark at Versailles, since by this time it was reaching the point of being substantially complete.

A pair of drawings by Liévin Cruyl, made shortly before January 1684, appear to suggest that from the start Louvois tried to assert himself and that he proposed plans, even at that early moment, which would have suggested the impact of his regime on the appearance of Versailles. Cruyl's drawings (Figs. 87 and 90) are dramatic bird's-eye views showing the château, the nearby town and gardens. They present certain unexecuted projects in the contemporary context. These include an early version of a great north wing symmetrical with the new south wing. There is also a grandiose project for a pair of large domed churches on either side of the château, and there is a spectacular new Orangery, a substantial amplification of earlier projects then under way.

With the possible exception of the north wing, which was carried out, but in a somewhat different form, the whole package of projects presented by Cruyl in this drawing was promptly rejected. In February work was undertaken on two churches, one the parish church, the other the Convent

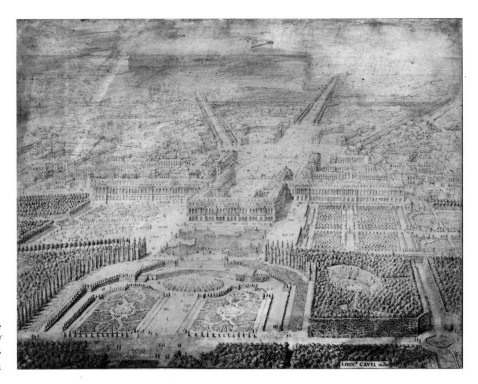

*90. Liévin Cruyl: bird's-eye
view of the palace of
Versailles seen from the
west. Drawing, dated 1684*

of the Recollets, which were constructed far from the great plaza before the
château where they appear in Cruyl's view. The Orangery project was also
rejected. Certainly this must have suggested how difficult change would be.

Louvois, however, deserves credit for embarking at once on a campaign
to enlist new talent. He decided immediately to try to obtain new works
from a sculptor from Marseilles, Pierre Puget, who had been little used by
Colbert. Puget had been employed by the state for more than a decade, but
through the ministry of the navy. In 1669–70 he was brought back to France
from Italy to oversee the design and execution of the massive sculptural
decoration of the ships of the line at the arsenal of Toulon. By 1683,
however, he had parted company with the navy in frustration and re-estab-
lished himself in Marseilles, feeling that his talents were unexploited by the
king.

A monumental piece of sculpture, reluctantly commissioned by Colbert,
stood for years in the tulip garden of the Toulon arsenal. It was a masterpiece, but it went unnoticed. Its enthusiastic reception at Versailles after its
chance discovery in 1683 clearly indicated Colbert's rigidity and failure to
make use of an artist remote from the group who worked regularly for the
king.

91. N. Bertin: *Pierre Puget's* Milo of Crotona *on its pedestal. Drawing*

Puget's statue is an over-life-sized representation of the great champion of the Olympic games, Milo of Crotona, shown being devoured by a lion because his hand had become caught in a tree stump (Fig. 91). The size of the statue and its powerful subject make it an unforgettable work, worthy of the grand aspirations of the king, and still capable of jolting visitors to the Puget Room of the Louvre out of their museum fatigue. Puget had also understood the basic principles and issues which most concerned the artists of the time. At a moment when Le Brun was lecturing on the expression of the human passions, Puget provided an *exemplum doloris* eventually to become a classic of French art.

Puget's work was clearly intended to recall the impact and the beauty of one of the most famous antiques in the Vatican, the *Laocoön* group. He had also illustrated a serious moral tale of the downfall of a proud man in ancient literature which had only rarely been depicted. (Milo's pride in his great strength had caused him to try to uproot the huge stump which caught his hand.)

After the unveiling of *Milo* Le Brun wrote to Puget: 'I tried to show His Majesty the many beauties of your work, but I was only doing you justice in doing this, since in truth this figure seems very beautiful to me in all its parts and worked with great art.'[30] Colbert had obviously missed an important opportunity.

Just ten days after Colbert died, however, Louvois wrote to Puget: 'The king having made me superintendent of the buildings, I ask you to reply whether you have any orders to make statues for the king and if you have, to tell me what they are . . .' A few weeks later, informed of several works at the Toulon arsenal or in Puget's hands, he remarked that he found *Milo* very beautiful and asked if Puget's age and health would allow him to work for some time. Puget was very excited by Louvois's interest and wrote a famous letter proposing a great equestrian group of the king and a 38-foot-high colossus for the canal of Versailles composed of six pieces of stone.

Puget must have understood the ambitions of the new superintendent when he thought to win him over by his most famous remark: 'I am nourished by great works, I submerge myself in them when I work [*je nage quand j'y travaille*]; and the marble trembles before me no matter how large the piece.'

One of Louvois's first great successes was the unveiling of a second Puget group, *Perseus and Andromeda* (Fig. 92), which the king liked even better than *Milo* and which appears to have sweetened the atmosphere of the art world of Versailles when Bernini's equestrian statue of the king, which arrived aboard the same boat, failed to please. Soon *Andromeda* and *Milo* were given places of honour in the garden flanking the entry of the great Allée Royale which led from the Latona parterre down to the canal.

Louvois learned promptly that the matter of making some personal impact on the vast enterprise of Versailles required both great tact and working within the system. In Puget he had typically chosen someone already partly established at court rather than fighting for a complete outsider.

92 (opposite). Pierre Puget: Perseus and Andromeda, formerly by the Allée Royale at Versailles. Marble sculpture

His general policy at the superintendency seems to have been to divide and conquer. What he rather rapidly managed was to sense the divisions of Colbert's organization and then gradually pull it apart along those lines in order to strengthen his own position. Of the three principal creative figures there, Le Brun, Le Nôtre and Hardouin-Mansart, Louvois mounted an attack against the first, exploited the great age of the second, pushing him towards retirement, and finally built an excellent relationship with the architect, whose enormous flexibility and tact allowed him to survive and even flourish under Louvois.

An attempt was made as early as December 1684 to bring about the disgrace of Le Brun and send him to the Bastille. The charges concerned misuse of funds at the Gobelins. Le Brun was saved by Louis; a situation similar to an armed truce prevailed until the painter's death in 1690.

Although Louis held Le Brun in the highest esteem, after the great work of the Hall of Mirrors was completed at the end of 1684, the painter lost his hold on his official positions. During Louvois's first year in office he interrupted the weaving of tapestries from Le Brun's cartoons at the Gobelins. By 1687 many of Le Brun's friends had deserted him, and Louvois's refusal of a picture offered as a gesture of conciliation the following year made it clear that a reconciliation between the two would never come about.

Mansart's much stronger position was already evident in February 1684, when a new building was undertaken, the parish church for the town of Versailles (Fig. 93). Though it is somewhat squat (because nothing was allowed to rival the château in height) and is distinctly grey, cold, stony, and lacking in the grace characteristic of most of Mansart's works, the decision to use his design shows that he was able to avoid the kind of harsh confrontation and near disaster which immediately faced Le Brun. One wonders, in fact, if the church was not intended to please Louvois by partaking of the austere style of military architecture erected by the likes of Vauban for Louvois as minister of the army.

A contemporary building in a similar mode proved to be one of the truly awesome works of the seventeenth century. This was the new Orangery (Fig. 89). On the planning boards when Louvois assumed the position of superintendent, its design must have been a matter of some controversy. By the end of the year 1684 the design had been completed, and it was realized for the most part during 1685 and completed in 1686 (Fig. 94). The scale of this venture is shown by the sums spent on it, particularly since most of the expenses were for the moving of earth and relatively simple masonry. In 1684, nearly half a million *livres* were spent; in 1685, 612 thousand.

There was an enormous interior, designed with sufficient elegance to

house activities during the part of the year when the oranges could be kept outdoors. Mansart's plan included a splendid domed vestibule at the end of one of the *allées* of the park and three great vaulted galleries, the longest of which (in the centre) was almost 500 feet long and nearly 30 feet high (Fig. 95). The outdoor staircases (Fig. 89) gained instant attention for their vast size and the impressive fact that each has one hundred steps. Colossal is the word for this greenhouse.

The resemblance between the Orangery and the military architecture of the time is very striking. The great arcades running around all three sides of the building (see Fig. 89) are similar to those often built behind the great walls of forts or the great courts of military buildings. Even the stone

93. Jules Hardouin-Mansart: Notre Dame, the parish church of the town of Versailles

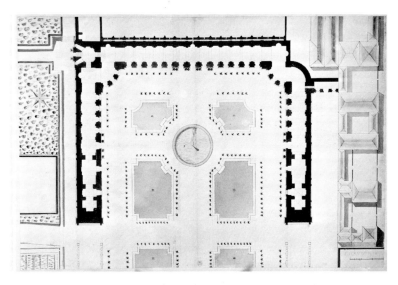

vaulting of the interior galleries is reminiscent of the passages found within the walls of forts except in scale.

It is not hard to imagine how the Mansart Orangery took on its special character. It was something of an engineering feat of terracing, and Louvois probably brought in his military architects for consultation. The giantism of the Orangery was perhaps the first concrete indication of the new policy of Louvois. Even before it reached completion other ambitious enterprises were undertaken, some of them almost wildly extravagant. To give a general idea of the scale of what went on one may return to the chart of the expenses for Versailles (Table 1, p. 50). The annual expenditures jumped from about 3,700,000 *livres* in 1683 to 11,300,000 *livres* in 1685!

By 1687 Mansart appears to have shared with Louvois the veto over all important architectural projects, not only at Versailles but in the whole of France. Louvois came to rely on Mansart's judgement in most instances.[31]

André Le Nôtre did less well than Mansart – in spite of some attributes which would have appeared to guarantee his position. He enjoyed such fame that Saint-Simon was able to say of him: 'he was celebrated for designing the fine gardens that adorn all France and have so lowered the reputation of Italian gardens ... that the most famous landscape architects of Italy now come to France to study and admire.' Such a man would have been hard to destroy for this reason alone. But Le Nôtre was also 'honest, honourable and plain-spoken; everybody loved and respected him ...' His relationship with the king went well beyond the respect earned by Le Brun; Louis allowed Le Nôtre to give him bear hugs. Shortly before Le Nôtre died, the king made the utterly unprecedented gesture of letting him visit the gardens carried in a chair next to him. He seems to have come as close to developing a personal friendship with Louis as any man ever did. There is no evidence that Le Nôtre's considerable age (he was past seventy) had in any way reduced his abilities.

Le Nôtre was too talented for his dismissal to be seriously considered. Mansart, for one, appears to have needed his talents. There is a tradition that it was Le Nôtre who supplied the broad lines of the solution of the difficult problems which surrounded the development of a satisfactory design for the Orangery. Certainly the building in its grand setting, with its magnificent proportions and unforgettable relationship to the southern axis of the park, suggests a final great work by the old man.[32]

Le Nôtre also designed for Louvois's Versailles a parterre which is a work of genius. The destruction of the intricate *parterre d'eau* of 1674 (Fig. 90) – directly in front of the west façade of the central part of the palace – resulted in the design of the present arrangement of two reflecting pools on either side of a new central walk. This new *parterre d'eau* carried the great

94 (above opposite). *Plan of the second Orangery of Versailles (Cabinet des Estampes Va. 423, tome 2). Drawing, after 1683*

95 (below opposite). *The long gallery on the east-west axis of the Orangery, looking east. Versailles*

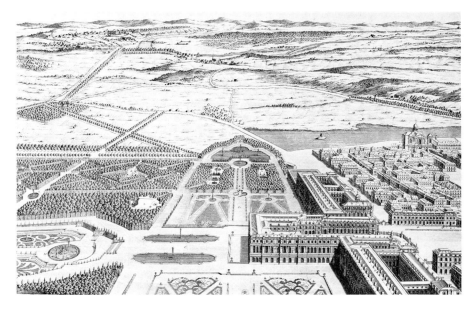

96. Dumas: a bird's-eye view of Versailles, detail. Engraving, one of six plates which represent a vast panorama seen from the south, after 1700

western axis of the garden right up to the palace (Fig. 96), perfecting the most remarkable element of the Versailles gardens. The beauty of Le Nôtre's design of the basins themselves (Fig. 97), with just enough curving of the

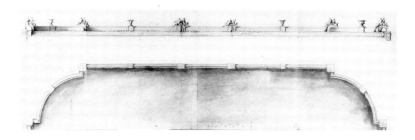

97. Plan and elevation of a project for the parterre d'eau (west parterre) of Versailles. Drawing, c. 1684

corners to add visual interest and grace to the conception while using monumentally simple elements consistent with the grandeur of the palace and park, represents his work at its best.

Though certainly conceived in its broad lines by Le Nôtre, the *parterre d'eau* design was modified by Mansart and possibly even by Mignard. An early plan shows the basins decorated with baskets and/or urns of sculptured flowers. Later these were transformed into groups of standing putti interspersed with reclining river gods (Fig. 117). This kind of collaborative planning, though not new, was especially symptomatic at this moment.

Le Nôtre seems to have ultimately been defeated by the character of the

98. Workshop of Mansart: project for the Colonnade bosquet *at Versailles* (T.H.C. 9). Drawing, c. 1685

institutions which he had helped to create. As the ensemble of park, palace and the surroundings (including the town) of Versailles were increasingly integrated, the thin line between architecture and garden became increasingly blurred, and the idea of garden planning as an activity quite separate from the designing of buildings seemed to be more and more difficult to defend.

The story of Mansart's Colonnade of 1685 (Fig. 98) seems to convey the nature of Le Nôtre's situation under Louvois. The Duke de Saint-Simon, in a somewhat jumbled account, records a famous remark of Le Nôtre made while viewing the Colonnade with the king: 'Well, Sire, what would you have me say? You have turned a stone-mason [Mansart] into a gardener and he has treated you to one of the tricks of his trade.' A look at Mansart's masterpiece might suggest either that Le Nôtre had poor judgement or that he was too attached to an old, archaic approach to appreciate a novel work.

99. The Salle de Bal, a bosquet in the gardens, 1681–3. Versailles

But a more satisfactory answer is that Le Nôtre was anxious above all to defend the integrity of garden design and to prevent its absorption by the architectural bureaucracy.

Perhaps the most important fact about the Colonnade, however, is that it was clearly the first work to be done without Le Nôtre's assent and advice. Thus it represented a serious intrusion into his area of authority and marked the imminent end of his activity. The old man still had certain great works to complete, most notably as a part of the rebuilding and updating of the Trianon in 1687, but even there it is difficult definitively to assign to him many of the parts. Le Nôtre did not suddenly disappear; he seems to have slowly faded away.

The Colonnade not only signalled the beginning of the decline of Le Nôtre's importance at Versailles, but was a very important enterprise in its own right. The project was much worked over and only later gained its present architectural character in which the figural sculptural decoration was restricted to the walls of the building (see Fig. 98).[33]

The style of the Colonnade can be characterized as light and graceful; indeed its elegance contrasts strikingly with the heavy ornamentation and rustication of most of Le Nôtre's works in this vein, such as the Salle de Bal (Fig. 99). The Colonnade strikes us today as a remarkable prefiguration of the architecture of the early eighteenth century, and it is certainly one of Mansart's most 'advanced' works. It is also worth noting the contrast between this structure and the other works of Mansart under way at this moment, namely, the Orangery and the parish church done in a 'military' style. Mansart did not just bring masonry to the garden. He was in search of something both appropriate and novel. The new regime clearly wanted to try new things, and despaired of teaching an old dog new tricks. It was probably less animosity than new ambitions which caused the superintendent to gradually move Le Nôtre towards his retirement.

A description of the role of Mignard at Versailles can perhaps round out this discussion of the changes in personnel which the ascent of Louvois in the arts administration produced. On the whole, the new superintendent was not extremely successful in advancing the cause of this artistic ally. He did manage to obtain for him the position of supervisor over certain sculptural projects, but it is not even certain that Mignard furnished the drawings for these, as Le Brun had done for similar works earlier in the decade. And while Mignard eventually took over Le Brun's position as First Painter of the king, director of the Academy of Painting and head of the Gobelins manufactory, this took place only after the death of Le Brun in 1690. It was perhaps typical of the difficult situation in which Mignard found himself that when Louvois stopped the weaving of tapestries after Le Brun's cartoons, it proved impossible to use Mignard's designs; other painters were engaged to do the *Sujets de la Fable* series which was commissioned. When Louvois arranged to have tapestry cartoons made at the Gobelins of two of Mignard's mythological scenes the superintendent agreed to pay for the weaving himself. He was reimbursed only in 1689 after Le Brun had left the Gobelins.

But Mignard did in fact land one very important commission, the painting of the large ceiling of the Petite Galerie (Fig. 100). This room was located above the vestibule of the Stairway of the Ambassadors and overlooked the main court of the château. It had formerly been part of the residence of Madame de Montespan, but since she was no longer the mistress of the king, it was reassigned to become an addition to the king's apartment. Louvois appears to have grasped the fact that this area provided a highly visible rival to the Grand Apartment, Colbert's recent triumph. Since Mignard's gallery for the king's brother at Saint Cloud had been much admired he was the natural candidate. And Louvois succeeded in getting him the commission.

Mignard was first paid in 1685 and in spite of his great age appears to have worked very quickly, eventually producing one of his finest works. Louvois lost no time proclaiming this success, since Audran's engravings of the ceiling (Fig. 100) were published in 1686, almost to coincide with the unveiling, rather than years later, as was usual. The ceiling itself is something of a surprise and, like the Colonnade, appears to suggest a new style for Versailles and a new era in French art. The subject was not very original: Minerva, the goddess of wisdom, crowns a child holding a bunch of lilies who symbolizes France, while Apollo (Louis's device) distributes presents to children and to women who represent the arts and the sciences. But the

100. Pierre Mignard: the (destroyed) ceiling of the Petite Galerie. Engraving by Audran, 1686

101. *An elevation of a project for the wall decorations of the Petite Galerie and two neighbouring salons at Versailles, possibly for the interiors set up at the Gobelins prior to installation in 1687*

work had charm, its most characteristic feature being the use of numerous putti decoratively carrying garlands of flowers and branches of leaves.

The framework of architecture into which Mignard's historical and decorative human figures were set is perhaps the most remarkable feature of the design. Compared with that of the Hall of Mirrors the ceiling is both simpler and flatter. The most striking aspect of Mignard's feigned architecture is the delicacy of the ornament. The whole would not have been out of place during the next century. In the Petite Galerie Mignard developed a kind of interior architectural ornament which looks forward to the works of Robert de Cotte and Lassurance.

Both the *Sujets de la Fable* (Fig. 102) and Mignard's ceiling are remarkable for their attempt at charm rather than emulating the grandly heroic tendency of most of the earlier painted decorations for Versailles. Both appear to share a simplicity and legibility of composition which contrast with the dramatic power and complex space of Le Brun's ceiling of the Hall of Mirrors.

The *Sujets* tapestries, though based on some drawings thought to be by Raphael and on others by Raphael's famous student, Giulio Romano, were graceful and featured attractive nude figures diverting themselves in bucolic settings. Most of the set was based on Romano's compositions for the Room of Psyche in the Palazzo del Tè in Mantua, depicting mythological fairy tales rather than great events of contemporary, biblical or classical history.

During Louvois's time the most important single project for Versailles was the permanent chapel which was to rise as the principal element of the new north wing (Fig. 103). The politics of religion were very prominent at this time. The persecution of the Protestants and the consequent revocation of the Edict of Nantes are very well-known; within the Catholic church too, much was going on, including the fight against such heresies as Jansenism, and Louis was engaged in a struggle against the power of the popes over the French church. Under these circumstances the residence of the French king demanded an imposing church, not just a temporary chapel.

102 (opposite). *After Alexandre Ubelski:* Dance of a Nymph, *designed after a drawing of the School of Raphael. Tapestry, c. 1686*

103. Plan of the Premier Étage of the château and palace of Versailles (T.H.C. 3). Drawing, c. 1687

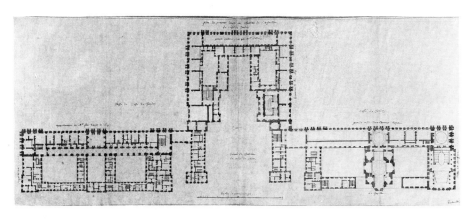

Mansart's first idea was to construct a vast domed building in the centre of the new north wing. The structure (Fig. 104) so resembled contemporary designs for the Dôme des Invalides that certain plans and elevations for the Invalides have been mistaken for it.[34] It also resembled in a very general way the great domed churches of Rome and of the papacy. Probably for nationalistic reasons the first design was scrapped. Instead it was decided to use the traditional form of the royal chapels of France, and work was begun in 1688 on a building which in its plan resembled the Sainte Chapelle at the Conciergerie in Paris, the chapels of the château of Vincennes, and Saint Germain-en-Laye (see Fig. 136). These churches were French Gothic in style. The new form posed many problems for architects trained primarily in the classical traditions of Italian Renaissance art, but it proved in fact to be the kind of problem which tested and proved the mettle of Mansart and the architects of the superintendency.

The surprisingly inventive quality of the design of Louvois's time has perhaps been underrated. Emphasis has mostly been on the enormous size and expense of the undertakings of these years; but it should also be stressed that this was in many ways a kind of golden age, with a large group of well-trained and gifted artists creating major works. (For the rest of the history of the Chapelle Royale, see Chapter 14, pp. 195 ff.)

The combination of a highly competitive environment, solid training and the evolution of a consensus about artistic values produced results that were often of considerable originality. The search for a Louvois style may well have played a role in the development of a French national style, one remarkable in its liberation from the dominance of the basically Italian standard of Le Brun and Colbert.

104. Cross-section of a discarded project for a chapel for Versailles (C.C. 2210). Drawing, c. 1686

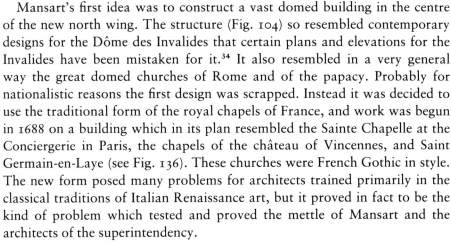

GRAND TRIANON

(1687)

T he greatest achievement of the King's Buildings Office during the superintendency of Louvois was the completion of a new royal palace in the park of Versailles. It replaced a charming pavilion covered with ceramics erected at Trianon during the 1670s for the enjoyment of flowers (Fig. 105).

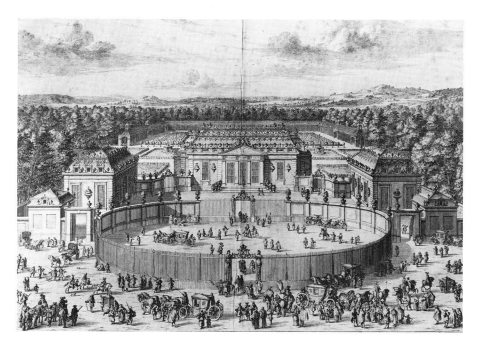

105. The Trianon de Porcelaine seen from the east (entrance side), built 1670-72. Engraving by Swidde, dated 1684

In this instance work proceeded with incredible speed, and the completion of the building must have seemed almost magical, apparently symbolizing the fact that with a wave of his hand Louis could cause the creation of a masterpiece of architecture. It is not known just when the first plans were drawn up, or even when the decision was made to begin construction, but payments indicate that work transforming the earlier building began in July of 1687. All the forces of the crown were then mobilized. As walls and windows rose at Trianon, the curtains to hang on them were being woven in Lyons, and at the royal manufactories old furniture was being restored and new made to fill the rooms. The king hovered over this enterprise, making frequent, almost daily, visits. He left on his traditional autumn visit to Fontainebleau with reluctance, and when he returned to Versailles on 13 November, he found the building quite advanced, though still not habitable. Nonetheless, Louis dined there for the first time on 22 January 1688 – seven months after work had begun.

The Trianon palace is concrete evidence of Louvois's incredible ability to get things done quickly and of the Buildings Office at work in top form. The aesthetic results were such as to allow for the immediate public proclamation that the place was a small masterpiece, another in the series of Louis's great triumphs as a builder. The elevations of the garden façades (particularly the west; Fig. 106) have at times been considered among Hardouin-Mansart's greatest achievements, the arcades and colonnades being seen as models of their kind.

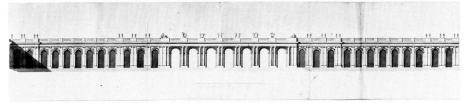

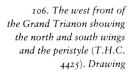

106. The west front of the Grand Trianon showing the north and south wings and the peristyle (T.H.C. 4425). Drawing

The Trianon is not, however, the brilliantly integrated and harmonious work sprung from the head of Mansart that has often been suggested. The plan of the new Trianon is surprising at least, if not actually incoherent. 'Neither a château nor a palace, it is also no villa or casino. It has the elevation of an orangery, the plan of a warren and is made of the materials of a royal house'.[35] This confusion is brilliantly masked by the incontestable seductiveness of the place.

Letters written by Louvois to Mansart, who was spending the summer of 1687 visiting distant spas for his health, show that little of what now stands can be connected to designs by the architect. Instead it is clear that the designs for the Grand Trianon evolved in a complicated dialogue between the patron and the lesser persons of the King's Buildings Office, and that the building's history is very complicated.

The story of the new Trianon is typical of much of the building history of Versailles. Some striking parallels to the history of the Enveloppe exist at Trianon, the most important being the attempt to create a design that would save as much of the pre-existing building as possible – while hiding the fact. There was also an awkward episode in which an early project was abandoned, walls pulled down or considerably altered, and a later project eventually completed.

The problems with the first plans must have asserted themselves almost at once, since even an outsider visiting the site in 1687 was dismayed by what he saw. The Swedish royal architect Nicodemus Tessin the Younger wrote the following in his travel journal during his stay in France:

I was at Trianon several times, twice with M. Le Nôtre, where the new château grew with great energy; the central portion [*corps de logis*] was knocked down for a second time while I was there, and it seems highly likely that nothing of value will ever rise. The building is only one storey high, and above it a raised roof *à la* Mansard rises above a balustrade. The frieze and pilasters are made of marble of a red-brown and yellow colour, the Ionic capitals and bases are of white marble; all the rest is made of common stone, all this clashes in a most disagreeable manner ... The garden façade is more than 200 *aulnes* long and is extremely irregular because of the gallery which is constructed with one of its sides by the small marsh.

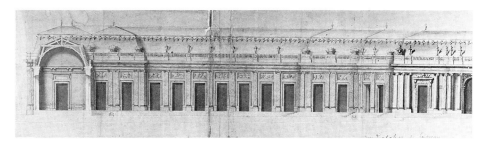

107. Elevation of a partly executed project for the Grand Trianon with a roof à la Mansard. Drawing, 1687

The central area appears to have been pulled down at least three times.

The king also appears to have been highly critical of the effect of the elevation of the building. On 18 September 1687 Louvois wrote to Mansart: 'His Majesty did not wish that we continue to put up the sloped roof, which he found looks too heavy and to give the Trianon palace the air of an enlarged house [*grosse maison*] ...'

These failed projects are known today in both plans and a partial elevation (Fig. 107) and the effect of what Mansart proposed was very much a patched-up job. The sloped roof was at first retained, because the old pavilions which were to be conserved had such roofs. The early projects appear to have been designed without a full formulation of the intention and function of the rooms of the new palace. The curious shape of the building (mentioned above by Tessin) was due to the king's wish to give

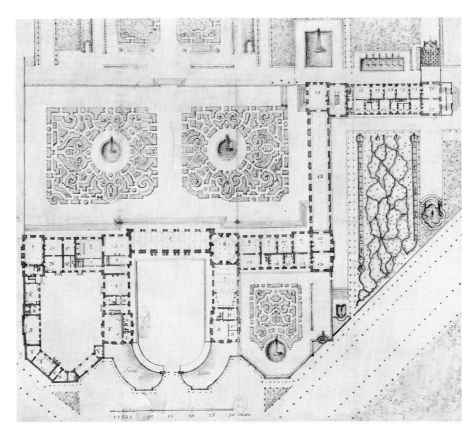

108. Plan of the Grand
Trianon (Cabinet des
Estampes Va. 424).
Drawing, c. 1687

permanent architectural form to aspects of the old Trianon complex which related to his movements and activities there. The gallery (Fig. 108, No. 13) replaced a favourite trellis walk of the king.

The invention of the peristyle (Figs. 106 and 108, No. 5), perhaps the most novel aspect of the palace as built (a structure still unplanned at the time of Tessin's visit), appears to represent a revision of the early plans directly related to a concern with the function of Trianon. In the early plans the preservation of the central pavilion had produced a very strange configuration (Fig. 109), a structure which bulged out awkwardly in the middle of the central façade. Furthermore, the central projection interfered with the view from the king's apartment. This element was eventually suppressed and replaced by a simpler large rectangular space (see Fig. 108, No. 5), joining the two former side pavilions of the old Trianon and providing the most direct possible connection between the right and left portions of the palace, and between the entry court and the garden (see Fig. 110).

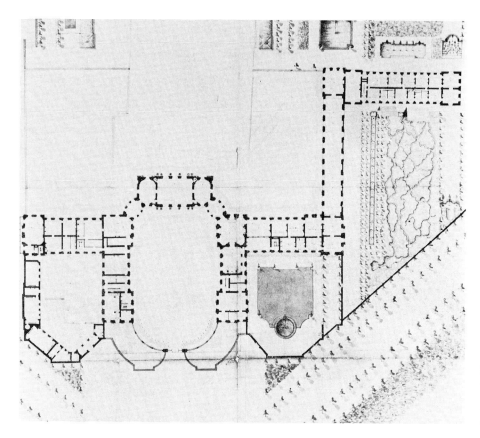

109. Plan of the Grand Trianon with the central pavilion of the Trianon de Porcelaine preserved (Cabinet des Estampes Va. 448 f). Drawing (now lost), 1687

As the peristyle was originally built it consisted of one long wall of French doors giving on to the court which was the principal entrance of the palace; most strikingly, the west wall was a colonnade creating a kind of garden room. This area has been described as Italianate. But the real interest of the peristyle lies in the manner in which its designer has simultaneously solved a number of problems while enhancing the beauty of the entire structure.

The peristyle is an archetypal element of the traditions of design at Versailles in at least one of its aspects. The concept developed not from the various Italian models often advanced to explain it, such as the Loggia of the Palazzo del Tè in Mantua or a loggia of the Villa Mondragone at Frascati, but rather from a French model of the 1670s for the château of Versailles itself.

Writers on Trianon seem to have forgotten that the ground-floor gallery of the Enveloppe palace, located, like the peristyle, in the central area

directly connecting the arrival court and the garden, was open to the elements. Furthermore, a monumental project for a vestibule designed to replace the original terrace on the west front included not only an open arcade on the ground floor, but a loggia with columns opening off the second-storey level of the three-storey-high vestibule as well (Fig. 111). This project contains, in aggrandized form, the same rectangular vestibule fully open on one side to the garden.

110 (opposite). Pierre Denis Martin: the Grand Trianon as built (M.V. 760). Painting, after 1700

111. Elevation of a large vestibule for the château of Versailles, a rejected project which appears on the same sheet as our Fig. 42. Coloured drawing, 1670s

The peristyle must be seen as a late phase in the planning, one in which the functioning of the building played the dominant role in its design. Considerable ingenuity produced a building removing the king from the ceremony and ritual of the court. Originally the king's private apartment at Trianon was put right up front by the main entrance, and the more public rooms such as the Salon du Jardin, which contained a billiard table, and the gallery, which seems to have been designed primarily for large card parties, were located far from the principal entry, diagonally across the garden. Also in a remote position requiring crossing of the king's apartment was the Trianon-sous-Bois, where the king's brother's family and others were to have their lodgings. This problem was fully solved only after 1703, when Louis moved into rooms running along the west side of a closed-back garden known as the Jardin du Roi. Nevertheless, the peristyle went a long way towards making Trianon work. The arriving visitor was pointed directly towards the garden paths and actually used these to reach most areas where members of the court could be received.

Not all of the ingenuity in the planning of the Trianon was lavished on the brilliant resolution of such functional problems. The Trianon disarmed most visitors. It proclaimed itself to be the palace of Flora, and although the room for smelling flowers of the Trianon de Porcelaine was transformed into a billiard parlour, the theme of garden palace still resounded throughout, particularly in the pictorial decoration. Choice landscapes from the royal collection were hung, and series of charming pictures depicting the metamorphoses of humans into flowers were commissioned. The gallery was eventually decorated with a remarkable series of large pictures showing the principal fountains and parterres of the park of Versailles (Fig. 112).

Two elements, the Trianon-sous-Bois and the Garden of the Springs (*Les Sources*), represent remarkable innovations. The idea apparently was that the Trianon-sous-Bois should literally be submerged in the woods. In 1694 Le Nôtre remarked to Tessin that the principal rooms were carefully related to major elements of the wooded garden around the Trianon-sous-Bois wing, and he made clear that a major aim of the design was the appreciation of the surrounding foliage and waters. Madame, Louis's German sister-in-law, whose famous letters to an endless number of German relatives frequently emerged from Trianon-sous-Bois, spoke of the branches of the trees as practically bursting into her rooms. It is generally said of the gardens of Versailles that a kind of geometric ordering, highly architectural in character, was applied to nature. Clearly the landscape of Trianon-sous-Bois and its relationship to the building were supposed to be something quite different.

The Garden of the Springs probably came about as a result of the marshy terrain of that corner of the park. In one of the more imaginative moments of Le Nôtre's splendid career he decided to save old trees and even something of the marsh itself, creating an irregular parterre crisscrossed with meandering springs (the plan of this is clearly visible on the right-hand side of Fig. 108). This design, which was developed from a less successful *bosquet* by Le Nôtre at Versailles, has even been seen as a kind of miniature forerunner of the English-garden style of the next century. It was clearly intended to be a delicious place to keep cool in hot weather and even a spot

112. The gallery of the Grand Trianon. c. 1687

for picnic-like lunches under the trees. *Les Sources* was certainly a bit of the charming ambience of the eighteenth century *avant la lettre*.

One of the most striking aspects in the history of designing the Trianon palace was the manner in which design decisions made largely for pragmatic and practical reasons were frequently turned to advantage and exploited for their novelty. The transformation of the marshy land into the Springs Parterre is a case in point, but an even more famous example and an equally novel one was the adoption of the Trianon 'white decor' for all of the walls made of wood and plaster (Fig. 112). Whether it was because the finishing of the interiors of the new palace coincided with a serious international crisis which called for the diversion of some funds from the completion of the palace, or simply that Trianon was intended to contrast sharply with the heavy grandeur of the Apartments at Versailles, or even that the king wanted the fastest possible completion of work (and all of these points may have played a role), Louis apparently said 'Paint everything white. No gilt or colour for the walls of Trianon.' The new white decor came at a time when the architectural articulation of the interior walls (e.g. panels, friezes, pilasters and column elements) had reached a new level of refinement in the hands of Mansart's expert in this speciality, Lassurance.[36] The overall schemes took on a refined grandeur, while a lightening of feeling was achieved by the increasing delicacy of purely decorative elements such as floral and architectural ornament.

A surprising message emerges from some of these elements in the design of Trianon. The old adage 'haste makes waste' may well apply here; certainly much money was wasted in pulling down poorly planned elements of the Trianon building. But, curiously, the designers of Versailles also seem to have been pushed to perform at their best and to do some of their most original work in this atmosphere of frequent semi-improvisation. Perhaps the rapid pace and necessary expediency of the creation of Trianon permitted a certain relaxation of the rules of high architecture which circumscribed work elsewhere.

An equally important message may also be that Trianon was created at a kind of moment of perfection in French art, one when the administrative strengths of Louvois's regime were admirably linked with the increasingly creative powers of the designers of the King's Buildings Office, and the result is, in fact, a kind of miracle, one which may well have proceeded from the growing mutual respect of the creative and administrative forces of Louis's government.

TECHNOLOGY

While Louis XIV was deeply concerned with the artistic evolution of Versailles, he also believed that the great monument he was building must be a triumph of technology. Among the legends of his court are numerous stories telling of inventors being granted audiences while ministers waited outside to discuss important matters of state.

Unfortunately, the documentation of this important aspect of the history of Versailles has for the most part disappeared. Papers relating to the administration of the Buildings Office, such as all payments, have been carefully preserved and exist in the archives, but most of the working memos and plans of the contractors have gone without a trace. We know much more about what was done than how it was accomplished. Furthermore, no systematic study has ever been published of the building techniques evident in what is still standing today, though this would shed useful light on the history of the building of Versailles.

Here and there, however, a striking fact emerges from the documents. The history of the repairs to the château during the eighteenth century is a case in point. It was discovered that the walls of the north and south wings were built not of solid masonry but of a combination of masonry and soft fill. Over the years the interior fill had settled, and by the second half of the eighteenth century the walls had become hollow in approximately the upper third of their height. The refilling of the walls entailed very substantial expenditure. The hollow walls were almost certainly the result of experimentation with new techniques which later proved faulty.

One case of an innovative modern technique was well known at the time of its use, about 1678. Since the Stairway of the Ambassadors (Fig. 7) had for reasons of convenience been located in an interior room without windows in the walls, the decision was made to use a large glass skylight for illumination. A structure of cast bronze was made to support the glass ceiling. The area of glass consequently was remarkably large. This technological triumph was certainly experimental in nature, and ultimately failed.

When the bronze supports weakened (near the middle of the eighteenth century) it was necessary to destroy the whole stairway and its remarkable paintings.[37]

A word should also be said about the continual invention in France of many small devices which refined the mechanics of building and made buildings both more comfortable and more secure. In the 1670s the marble floors of the King's Grand Apartment leaked downstairs when washed, and the decision was made to replace them with wood. Thus the *Parquet de Versailles* was invented, a treatment of hard wood flooring which was to remain classic (see Fig. 11).

Cronström, the representative of the Swedish royal architect, was carefully instructed to keep Stockholm fully informed of all new details of new building hardware in France, such as locks, window hooks and even curtain rods, the assumption being that innovation in these areas was more or less constant in France and should be promptly imitated.

In 1693 Cronström was very happy to be able to supply a drawing of the new hardware of the Hôtel de Seignelay for Tessin, the Swedish royal architect, and the drawing actually survives in Tessin's collection. In the five years since Tessin had last seen Paris, Cronström wrote, many refinements had been made in the area of locksmithery. He then remarked that the drawing he sent, which might seem beautiful, was in fact only a common work from the master who made it.

Knowledge of the use of technology is most complete where the construction of the gardens is concerned, particularly in the area of waterworks and canals. The earliest fully documented example of the deliberate use of scientific knowledge at Versailles concerns the beginning of the building of the Grand Canal. In 1672 the Abbé Picard and Philippe de la Hire of the Academy of Science studied the problems of the level of the canal when its enlargement and the construction of the crossing branches running from the Trianon to the zoo were being considered. Similar consultations were made for the construction of the great reservoirs such as that by the Avenue de Paris and one on the Satory hill to the south of the château.

The Francini family, hydraulic specialists, were a part of the Versailles team from an early date when they were transferred from work at other royal residences, such as the maintenance of the famous grotto fountains of Saint Germain-en-Laye. Several drawings survive among the papers of the royal architects and designers, mostly of pipelines, but occasionally also cross-sections of fountains, which suggest that this technological aspect of Versailles was closely integrated with the overall designing and planning of the château and its park.

The great bathroom on the ground floor, planned between 1669 and 1671,

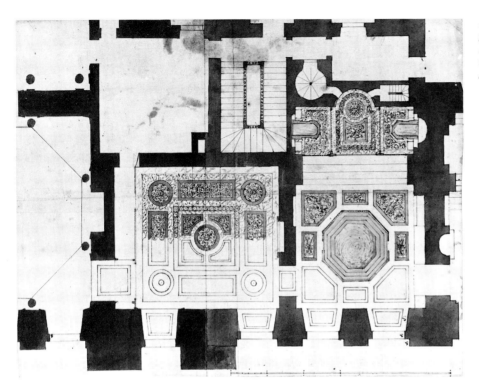

113. Ground plan of one project for the King's Bathroom at Versailles (C.C. 397). Coloured drawing, c. 1671

was certainly intended to indicate that modern technology was at the service of the pleasure of his majesty. There was a great sunken pool (Fig. 113) and also two enormous tubs. Running hot and cold water were available. So important was the royal bath that it was one of the special rooms for which

114. Charles Le Brun: tritons and nereids, project of a relief decoration for the King's Bathroom at Versailles (G.M. 8226)

the painter Le Brun himself was asked to provide the designs for the ornamental sculpture (Fig. 114).

Hot-air heating was also tried at Versailles: apparently the warming devices attached to the water heaters of the king's bath were used to heat the air.

Many years later, and far away from running water, a hot-air heating device was even considered for the new bedroom of the ailing old king, built in 1701. Since this system was never mentioned by such observant visitors as Cronström, it is fair to presume that the method used upstairs did not prove very successful. The warm bathroom, however, must have seemed a triumph of modern technology during the early 1670s, when the bath was still a novelty.

It was later, during the last years of the 1670s (and during Louvois's regime), that questions of technology, especially those related to the bringing of water to Versailles, became almost an obsession of the king. The growth of the palace and the multiplication of the fountains and other waterworks outpaced the ability of the hydraulic engineers to provide water. Several new reservoirs were built, and the hills around the château must have been dotted with many windmills to drive pumps. Still it was not possible to keep the existing fountains playing most of the day.

At one moment Louis apparently even considered giving up Versailles altogether for another spot better supplied with waters. The business of obtaining more water for Versailles thus became synonymous with the further development of the place. Obtaining water was certainly of equal importance to any artistic question at the time when Louvois took over the superintendency.

A partial estimate of the cost of two of the principal hydraulic projects for Versailles came to over 13 million *livres*. Some comparable figures will show how enormous an element this was in the overall expenditure. From 1664 to 1690 (thus including all the years of these hydraulic expenses, and almost another score of years as well), the total moneys spent for paintings, gilding and buying new pictures were about 1·7 million *livres*; all new sculptures during this period had cost about 2·7 million *livres*; and the pay of all day workers of the château and park amounted to only 1·3 million.

Charles Perrault wrote:

Everything that could possibly bring water to Versailles was so sacred and so well received by the king that ... [Colbert] listened to every project with an inconceivable equanimity and went to unbelievable troubles to verify everything which was proposed, even though most of the time these were the purest fantasies.

Not only quacks came before Colbert; given the enormous stakes, serious engineers evolved vast projects. The first of these came from Riquet, author of the greatest technical marvel of Louis's reign, the great Canal des Deux Mers, which joined the Atlantic Ocean with the Mediterranean. He suggested that the altitude of the great Loire river was such that a part of it might be brought to Versailles by the construction of a canal. Picard of the

Academy of Science revised Riquet's figures, showing that the Loire was in fact lower than Versailles at any feasible distance from which a canal could be built. However, this project brought forth a number of similar ones using other (presumably higher) rivers. The stream of the Gobelins at Bierre was considered. Charles Perrault also mentions that a proposal suggesting the diversion of the Étampes river towards Paris, which he saw as possible, could have provided almost limitless water for a new royal residence *other* than Versailles.

The decision to divert a river to Versailles was finally made when the greatest engineer of the era, Vauban, the famous builder of fortifications, showed that the diversion of a Norman river, the Eure, was possible from a point near Chartres or some forty miles away. In October 1684, just a year into Louvois's superintendency, the king decided to proceed. Thirty thousand troops, destined to depart for winter quarters, were suddenly conscripted to work for the contractor.

For a while it must have looked as if the superintendent was on the brink of one of the greatest triumphs of the reign. On 8 June 1685, Louvois was able to report to the king that 1,600 arches of the arcade of the aqueduct were rising, including some that were 'twice the height of the towers of Notre Dame' (Fig. 115). In September 1685, and again in July 1686, Louis

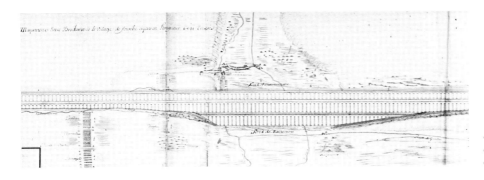

115. *Elevation of the great aqueduct of Maintenon, detail (C.C. 655). Drawing, c. 1684*

visited the region. 'The work goes quickly and success is assured,' wrote Dangeau. Between 1685 and 1688 the newspapers suggested that the river Eure excited great public interest.

The project eventually failed completely, at first owing to the unlucky presence of serious illness which decimated the workers and soldiers (this was even caught, though not fatally, by both Louvois and the king himself). But it was finally military necessity that brought a quick suspension to the works late in the spring of 1688.

That such a vast project was ever undertaken is surprising, but it is even

*116. The Marly Machine.
Engraving, c. 1686*

more so when it is recalled that two other enormous hydraulic undertakings were in progress at exactly the same time. The first was the famous Machine de Marly (Fig. 116), called the 'machine of the river Seine' by its inventor Arnold de Ville, an engineer from Liège. This was to supply the reservoirs of Versailles with water by purely mechanical means. Work on a vast structure by the Croissy Islands in the Seine went on for six years beginning in 1681. A whole dynasty of engineers, headed by Rennequin Sualem, accompanied de Ville south from Flanders, and the machine was mostly complete by 1682. Water from the Seine was eventually raised 470 feet. After the machine was completed, another year was required to build aqueducts between Marly and Versailles.

Everyone was overwhelmed with the success of the machine, which rapidly became known as one of the wonders of the age. The king gave de Ville the gift of 100,000 *livres* and a pension of eight thousand. Such lavish gratitude was at least in part due to the fact that the machine, in addition to providing much of the water desired by the king for Versailles, was also a much-needed cover-up for the failure of the project for the diversion of the river Eure.

During most of the 1680s, when neither of these grand projects was yet operational, still a third scheme, invented and perfected by more usual means within the context of the king's administration, was able to solve much of the need for more water. The third system, which employed a series of canals and aqueducts to bring water from high areas near Versailles to the reservoirs of the park, was carried to perfection by Thomas Gobert and Abbé Picard. It was perhaps the least recognized major accomplishment of the era. In as little as three years all kinds of systems for the collection of water were integrated, and by 1683 the park of Versailles was already adequately supplied. The work of Gobert and Picard is more interesting from every point of view than the Marly machine, though it was, and remains, hardly known, even to experts.[38]

Technology also played a role in the evolution of the figurative arts at Versailles, for instance, after December 1682, making a mark in the history of sculpture with the brothers Jean-Jacques and Jean-Balthazar Keller. They had been brought to France from Zurich to cast cannon and the like for Louvois, and had carried their craft to such a level that it was decided that they should begin to do sculptures eight to ten feet high. The first works for Versailles, made between 1684 and 1685, were four figures – *Apollo*, *Bacchus*, *Mercury* and *Silenus* – which are now set up on pedestals against the central garden façade of the château.

By 1687 the Kellers were producing real masterpieces, beginning with the splendid animal groups of Mansart's two water *cabinets* to the west of the new *parterre d'eau* (Fig. 120), and moving on to the many grand reclining figures of rivers and nymphs for the western *parterre d'eau*. These were modelled as early as 1686 (Coysevox dated his *Garonne* (Fig. 118) that year) but were not cast until between 1688 and 1690. In the end some fifty pieces were completed.

The introduction of bronze statuary into the gardens of Versailles profoundly altered the character of much of the garden. Near the château a marvellous contrast was developed between the lovely white marble of certain pieces such as Coysevox's and Tuby's grandiose Vases of Peace and War (1684; Fig. 119) and the dark material of the new sculptures. In this context even marble sculptures gained in value. Many of the twenty-four sculptures of Colbert's 1674 commission, which had just been completed,

117. The parterre d'eau, *Versailles. Photograph by Eugène Atget, July 1901*

118. Antoine Coysevox: The Garonne, *a river god. Sculpture, dated 1686, cast in bronze after 1688.*
Versailles, parterre d'eau

119. Antoine Coysevox:
the Vase of War
(illustrating the war against
the Turks in Hungary).
Marble sculpture, 1684.
Versailles, corner of the
palace terrace

120 (opposite). Martin
Desjardins: Diana (the
Evening, from the series
The Four Times of the
Day). Marble sculpture,
1680. Versailles, by the
north water cabinet

were available for use anywhere, since the parterre for which they had been designed was destroyed. These, such as Desjardins's masterpiece *Diana* (the *Evening*; Fig. 120), were set up against the trees and hedges around the edges of the western and northern parterres to striking effect. So handsome was this arrangement, in fact, that the decision was eventually made to decorate the lines of trees of most of the major axes of the park with sculpture groups. The Allée Royale, for example, was eventually completed by alternating marble statues with vases of the same material (Fig. 121). This proliferation of sculpture actually fulfilled an ambition of the designers of Versailles, which was to create a place where students of art could study the great masterpieces of ancient and contemporary sculpture, a new Rome of the north.

121 (opposite). *The Allée Royale, looking east (with the marble statue of* Cyparisse *by A. Flamen, 1696). Versailles*

VERSAILLES IN AN ERA
OF POLITICAL AND
MILITARY DISASTER

(1688–98)

The almost limitless projects on a grandiose scale characteristic of much of the 1680s were symptomatic of an important shift in the character of the French government, one which was to have very serious implications for the future of France and, in turn, for the history of Versailles. Earlier a somewhat precarious balance had always been maintained between the aims of the king and his ability to accomplish them. (During the 1660s and 1670s policy was formulated by setting goals that were admittedly ambitious but were reasonably likely to be achieved, given the considerable financial resources of the French state.) But after the first half of the 1670s, and especially after the death of Colbert in 1683, a change began to manifest itself. Pragmatism gradually gave way to more rigid attitudes. Principles were increasingly regarded as sacred. A new sense of unreality was certainly shown by the determined attempt of the French government to forget many of the dire financial consequences of the Dutch War of the 1670s.[39]

At the core of Louis's eventual undoing seems to have been his rigid religious policy. Whatever one's judgement of the morality of his religious actions in the 1680s, no one now doubts that France moved towards disaster as a result of them. With his revocation of Henry IV's Edict of Nantes the practice of the reformed religion was suddenly forbidden; all children were to be educated as Catholics, and a final cruel twist was added by the prohibition of Protestant emigration. About 50,000 French families, some of wealth and talent, fled anyway and inflamed international Protestant opinion with stories of atrocities.

Shortly before the revocation Louis began a quarrel with Innocent XI which ultimately resulted in Louis's excommunication and, finally, his successful defiance of the pope. The papacy had become one of Louis's most angry enemies. This double enmity defused the Protestant/Catholic religious issue which had dominated European politics for a century and a half, and facilitated the formation of a grand alliance of Catholic and Protestant powers against the French.

It appears that the French government never quite grasped the fact that military and political events were shifting rapidly to its extreme disadvantage. The turning back of the Turks at the siege of Vienna (1683) and the many victories of the Austrian empire gradually freed one of Louis's greatest enemies, the Emperor, to act against him. Furthermore, James II, a pro-French king, was immobilized by religious struggle in Britain, while William of Orange managed in 1686 to form an alliance of Austria, Spain, Bavaria, Saxony and the Palatinate, known as the League of Augsburg. When William became king of England in 1688 he added another important country to the League. A situation had developed which eventually blossomed into the great struggle which has been called the first world war.[40]

Louis and Louvois convinced themselves that the League was too divided to be effective and that the French military machinery was so superior to all others that the alliance might be dismembered by a swift and terrible military action. This mentality precipitated the invasion and devastation of the Palatinate (October 1688), a notorious early example of scorched-earth warfare.

Quite the opposite of bringing the allies to their knees before so great a military power, the blitzkrieg policy nearly bankrupted France. A long war began. By the end of November 1689, the French royal coffers were completely empty. It was uncertain how the army could be paid and supplied so that it could hold secure the frontiers of France (which were particularly vulnerable because they had been recognized by treaty only in 1684).

This great crisis of the reign was temporarily solved by the sacrifice of one of the wonders of Versailles, the solid silver furniture, and the plate for the royal table. The Marquis de Sourches wrote in his journal for 1 December 1689 an account of what happened:

We were certainly astonished when the king declared that he was going to send all of his silver to the mint to melt it, and we were extremely sad to see so large a number of admirable things which would be destroyed in one moment, beyond which it was an extreme loss since the making of them (quite apart from their material) had cost immense sums. But the king listened to none of these arguments, having decided that it was necessary for the good of his state ... he made his resolution with unequalled firmness.

Sourches continued that when Du Metz suggested that Colbert would have found a dozen ways to save the silver, Louis simply replied: 'Maybe, but not even one is to be found at this moment.' Louis eventually realized less than half of the six million *livres* he hoped from the melting, but he had enough to keep the army together and in the field for the moment.

The complete reorganization of the royal treasury which followed left insufficient funds for the maintenance of Versailles, much less for any new works. Draconian economies had taken place between the years 1688 and 1690 (see Table 1, p. 50). Expenses then were cut from about four-and-a-half million to less than four hundred thousand *livres*. By 1690 it was impossible even to honour old contracts. In July 1691 Louvois, the great mover of projects, died suddenly; the post went to a more ordinary administrator, Villacerf. It was he who was to preside over the disaster.

A valiant attempt to save face and to minimize the humiliation of the king was made. Sourches mentioned an important point. Louis could certainly have sold his furniture and other silver objects for several times the value of the metal. He refused to do so and to allow beautiful objects made for him to be acquired for the palaces of his enemies.

Credit, and the good-will of craftsmen and designers, who for the most part had few alternatives to royal patronage, were exploited as far as was possible to create impressive replacements for the noble objects which disappeared. Some remarks in Félibien's guide of 1703 seem to reflect the public posture of the government on the issue of the melting of the silver.

Although so many works of silver and gold were admired, today a large number of excellent workers could easily make similar things, and perhaps even more wonderful works ... what one sees [of various semi-precious stones] in the Gallery, its salons and in the apartments, seems to be highly valuable, both by the value of these oriental stones and by the extraordinary workmanship necessary to work all of these vases and all these excellent porphyry busts ...

Great art was used as a substitute for the earlier creations of the Gobelins. This was the first of the two principal strategies employed to maintain the brilliance of the king's residence. The royal collection of antique statuary was also widely used. Statues and busts with stone bases seem to have replaced many of the remarkable silver objects.[41]

For the replacement of the lost furniture, the decision was made to exploit the craftsmen of the realm, and they worked brilliantly with inexpensive materials.

In this context the art of embroidery seems to have come into its own and even to have reached new heights. Symbolic landscapes were frequently shown on the upholstery of seats. Silk thread and cloth were available at reasonable prices from royal manufactories and thus were not costly in terms of hard cash (4,148 *livres* were spent for embroideries over the years 1690–91, while only 2,632 *livres* went for gold thread[42]).

It has traditionally been suggested that the great inlaid furniture of C.-A. Boulle was developed at this period. A famous commode made for the king's bedroom at the Trianon around 1706 (Fig. 122) gives some idea of this Boulle style. The piece remains sculptural in shape, in the tradition of the silver furnishings of Versailles (see Fig. 79), but Boulle's work is made

122. *Charles-André Boulle: commode for the king's bedroom at the Grand Trianon. Ebony wood with inlays of exotic woods, tortoiseshell and gilt bronze with cast bronze gilt ornaments. c. 1706*

of exotic woods, gilt brass and tortoiseshell, mostly from the French colonies of America and Asia. Seeing Boulle's development as merely the result of the difficult times after 1690 is, however, simplistic; the quality of wood inlay work was already superb in the 1670s, as a cabinet recently acquired by the Getty Museum fully demonstrates (Fig. 123). But it does seem possible that the famous 'Style of Boulle', using a richly dark colour scheme, dominated by the tones of dark wood and shell and enlivened with gilt

metal, and with elaborate ornament featuring delicate lacy designs spread over most surfaces, could have developed as a response to the problems of the 1690s.

After the crisis of 1690, royal policy seems to have been to stress the idea of business as usual. Work resumed on certain areas of the Trianon. Mansart built a new gallery for the king's brother at the Palais Royale in Paris, and as soon as the worst of the cash flow crisis had passed by the end of 1691, thoughts turned once again to the embellishment of Versailles. Obviously, however, under the circumstances it was necessary to make a maximal effect at a minimal price.

A minor triumph was achieved by the ingenuity and talents of Louis's creative staff in 1692–3, as the Nouveau Bâtiment (Fig. 124) rose largely

123 (opposite). Gobelins manufactory: door panel from a cabinet representing the French cock triumphant over the eagle of the Empire and the lion of Spain. Inlay of various exotic and coloured woods. 1670s

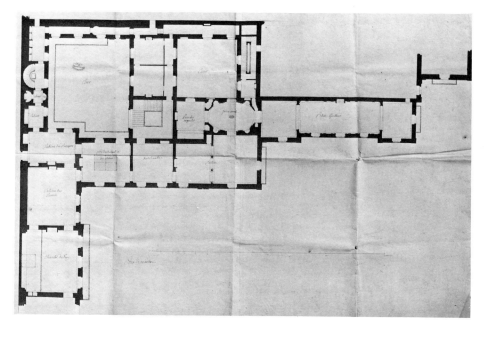

124. Floor plan of the Premier Étage of the old château of Versailles with the additions and changes of 1692, including the Oval Salon and next to it the Shell Room. Drawing, after 1701

within the walls of the château of Louis XIII. The work involved primarily four public rooms on the Premier Étage, two under the roof of the old château and two slightly smaller ones directly behind, extending into the northern interior court. The remainder of this new construction was rather unglamorous and utilitarian.

No urgent need can account for this 'New Building', though space was always short at Versailles; the function of these rooms was the display of works of art and collections of natural curiosities which could well have been displayed elsewhere. The intention was to use the king's large and brilliant collections to replace something of the vanished brilliance of the melted furniture. One of the new rooms was called the Shell Room, and the two rooms overlooking the main courtyard (below the Shell Room on the plan) are referred to in later guides (Piganol) as the Picture Cabinets. Works of Le Brun and Mignard, spiced with a few masterpieces of the Italians and Nicolas Poussin's *The Judgement of Solomon*, were distributed there. The area was actually a continuation of the Petite Galerie of the 1680s containing Mignard's famous ceiling (see Fig. 100).

An unusual element of the decoration was the Oval Salon (Fig. 126), which connected the picture rooms with Mignard's gallery. This room was not designed to show paintings but rather was conceived for the display of modern sculpture. A large bronze version of Girardon's equestrian statue of Louis XIV was set up in the centre. Niches in the walls provided a display area for four statues: Girardon's group of *Pluto abducting Persephone* (Fig. 125); Marsy and Flamin's *Abduction of Orithyia by Boreas*; and the great

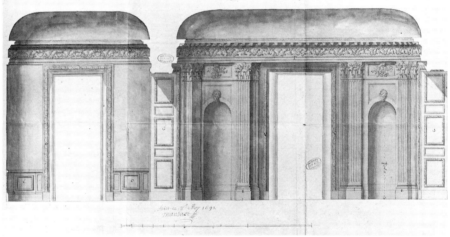

125. A pedestal made for the Oval Salon and the bronze reduction of François Girardon's Pluto abducting Persephone *which stood on it. Drawing*

126. Elevations of the north walls of the Oval Salon and the Shell Room at Versailles. Drawing, signed 'Mansart' and dated 3 May 1692

Italian groups (formerly firedogs) by Alessandro Algardi, *Jupiter* and *Juno*.

Hardouin-Mansart's team rose admirably to the challenge of designing a setting fully worthy of high art (Fig. 126). The complex and fragmented designs made for a new chamber for the king at the Grand Trianon in the same year gave way in the Oval Salon to a design of real architectural grandeur.[43] The graceful shape of the room and the elements which 'rose freely' upwards, coupled with the finely delicate design of the frieze, resulted in a masterpiece of interior design.

The New Building appears to represent a major change in French interior decoration. It is clear from the correspondence of the Swedish diplomat

Cronström that a complete change of taste had just taken place. On 19 April 1693 Cronström remarked:

> ... I should also tell you that most window and door frames are being made in white marble, because it is no longer the custom to paint [in colour] panelled rooms, doors, shutters ... ceilings ... etc., only white highlighted with gold lines or just plain white paint [is used]. Many even make these windows and door frames in wood painted white, with white marble being used only along the floor mouldings, and in certain panels directly above. Fireplaces which are both attractive and inexpensive have resulted from this practice.

Important drawings and fragments of paintings by Mignard made for the Oval Salon and the Shell Cabinet were never put in place. Louis's failure to hang these works was '... less a matter of money than taste ... the king preferred walls which he could hang with beautiful pictures, to painted ceilings.'[44]

*

The year 1694 proved the lowest point in the history of the arts under Louis XIV. On 7 May Daniel Cronström wrote to Nicodemus Tessin:

> ... I must inform you, sir, that all the funds for the workers of the Gobelins and the Galleries of the Louvre have been rescinded, that poverty and unemployment are general and that we can really hire the very best craftsmen in the world for next to nothing ... all the tapestry makers of the Gobelins, [the] Janse [weavers] etc. are on the point of asking for alms ... If the king [of Sweden] would like to have furniture or tapestries made, the cost will come to about half of what it would ordinarily.

Nor were things much better the next year; in April the departure for Poland of François Desportes, the animal and still-life painter, prompted Louis to forbid French artists to work abroad without the permission of Villacerf. As late as June of 1697 it was again necessary to take steps to control the 'brain drain' abroad of French artists; in an attempt to ensure the eventual return of artists working abroad, the king refused to allow their families to join them.

An almost pathetic note of Cronström's gives some idea of how bad things actually had become. In June 1697 he visited Louis's brother and sister-in-law at their château of Saint Cloud.

> I found that they were rather ashamed because we [in Sweden] do such great things in the way of royal buildings, while here [in France] it is only possible to do one hundredth of that. Recently twelve marble vases were made for [the château of] Marly, which made a considerable impression ...

After the separate peace treaty with Savoy was signed in May 1696, leading to the end of war in September 1697, there was some optimism about the state of the arts in France, but the French economy was in such poor condition that even peace made no immediate improvements. Almost a year after peace, in July 1698, Cronström wrote:

There is still no very substantial news about the arts here, although some attempt has been made to symbolize a revival by the opening of the Church of the Invalides [in Paris]. All the interior decoration has been halted since the beginning of this war, even that which had already been started, and now they are carrying out the same projects which were then approved. The number of glaziers and sculptors is so reduced [here] that this single project [*endroit*] is able to employ just about all the good sculptors of this city and [in fact] everyone is rushing there as to a fire because of the complete lack of work for the king and the few commissions from others.

This is not quite a fair picture of the state of affairs at the King's Buildings Office, since Louis appears to have celebrated the end of the war by deciding to undertake the construction of a great water work, the cascade, at his retreat a few miles from Versailles, the château of Marly. Moreover, in November 1698 the great Abreuvoir, or pool, at the bottom of the Marly garden was undertaken as well. Both of these structures set new standards of grandeur for the Marly garden. However, neither called for important works of art to keep the royal sculptors busy, and apparently they were not so significant as to appear of great importance to Monsieur and Madame.

After writing that the peace had brought few new projects, Cronström noted that Louis had made known his intention to make some changes in his Versailles apartment, particularly to make his bedroom more convenient and to create at the same time a new apartment near it for the Duke of Burgundy (next to that of the dead queen, where the duke's wife, Marie-Adélaïde, was sleeping). But it took a year for the plans to be finalized and work to begin.

The principal creative activity of 1698 was the formulation of plans and the beginning of work on the summer and winter apartments at the zoo for the Duchess of Burgundy. The search for somewhere to build a pet house for the little girl had not proved successful, so Louis decided to give this favourite child his own zoo and redecorate it for her.

The decorations of the zoo would be famous in the history of Versailles if for no other reason than the king's remarks about them. In a typically grand act Louis rejected out of hand the programme of subjects proposed for the ceiling decorations of the new rooms. His famous marginal comment on Mansart's programme characterized the concept as old-fashioned and demanded that something with more youth in it be devised. Mansart's idea had been to represent on each ceiling a god or goddess suitable for the room, *à la* Versailles.[45]

The elevations of the elegantly designed walls of the zoo pavilion are well known from many drawings (Fig. 127), but the painted programme and the final character of the place are not. Presumably a simple white and gold decor existed when the king first visited the partially completed rooms in January 1700; later Claude III Audran seems to have provided important paintings, but these are not known.

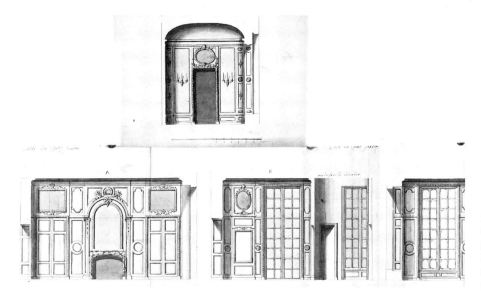

127. Elevations of some walls of rooms redecorated for the Duchess of Burgundy at the Versailles zoo (Ménagerie). Drawing, 1698

The elevation drawings of the walls are highly innovative, and it has even been argued that they presuppose a steady evolution in style over the war years which appears to have taken place in spite of the lack of commissions.[46] The implication of these fine drawings is that the art of design in France did not suffer important reverses after the closing of the Gobelins, and that even after the catastrophic years of the 1690s there was potential for the restoration of the arts to their earlier brilliance.

THE LAST GREAT
WORKS

(1699–1711)

1699 began on a very auspicious note. Cronström announced to Tessin in a letter from Paris dated 2 January that the Gobelins was about to reopen, or, more precisely, that the French king had made funds available to complete those tapestry projects which had been halted by the war. He ended the passage with the phrase '... all is to be resumed again at the manufactory.'

On 6 January Cronström had more important news. He told Tessin that a fundamental reorganization of the King's Buildings Office was taking place and that in an unprecedented move the first architect, Hardouin-Mansart, had been appointed to the ministerial position of superintendent, thus becoming the successor of Colbert and Louvois. Cronström reported further that Mansart had effectively run things under his predecessor Villacerf, and he commented: '... it [Mansart's] is one of the great fortunes that has been seen to have been made in France.'

Cronström wrote again to Tessin on 8 January with more exciting news. 'They are saying that he [Mansart] will begin his superintendency with the [new] chapel and the [new] theatre of Versailles, and with the great [high] altar [for Notre Dame de Paris] whose construction was ordered by Louis XIII.' Work started almost at once on the chapel; payments indicate that before the end of January part of the foundations for a previous chapel project (which had been laid down just before the war at the end of the 1680s) was torn up to make room for the foundations of another design. The first months of the superintendency seem to have been almost frantically busy.

Early in 1699 a number of projects were considered and some few undertaken for the gardens of Versailles. On 25 January designs were requested for a new *bosquet* for the empty spot called the *sablonnière* below the north-west corner of the *parterre d'eau*. By February really grand things were being considered in the way of sculptural programmes. A project for mythological figures to make the basin at the end of the northern axis of the garden into the Basin of Neptune was about to be reviewed, as well as another for large groups of figures for the centres of the two basins of the *parterre d'eau* in front of the west façade of the château. Nothing was to come of these sculptural enterprises, but in the spring the Bosquet de la Renommé was redesigned and a new *bosquet* was built which included a kind of pavilion to hold the great sculptures of *Apollo and the Muses* and the horses of Apollo (see Fig. 45), formerly in the Grotto of Thetis, which had been moved to the Renommé in 1684.

Some garden projects of this period provide a clear documentation of the high level of taste of the moment and of a decisive move away from grandeur towards a new delicacy. On 11 February Louis asked that the metal grilles in the walls of the Petit Parc be replaced. According to Mansart's journal he specifically demanded that the new gates should be of the 'delicacy of those of Meudon' (the old residence of Louvois, which was being refurbished for the dauphin). These gates do not survive, but some drawings for the redecoration of the Meudon interior do (Fig. 128), and they give some idea of its decorative style. Fantasy, charm, delicacy and arabesque curves, based on Roman plaster ornamentation in the mode of the ruined Golden House of Nero in Rome, are the vocabulary of Meudon. Louis's citing of designs for Meudon as models for Versailles is surprising and unprecedented, in that he appears to be following the taste of another for the first time.

The immediate response of the Mansart group to the king's admonition is not quite clear, but it seems likely that a style based on the art of Jean Bérain,[47] head of Louis's *Menus Plaisirs* (designers of temporary *fête* and stage designs), carried the day. The reaction of the Mansart workshop to Louis's demand can be judged from the exactly contemporary redecoration of the King's Bedchamber at Marly. A drawing for a central ceiling ornament (Fig. 129) shows that a feeling had developed for gentle arabesque curves, and small, rather delicate shapes.

At the same time Louis was commissioning other very important works for Marly (Fig. 130). The decision was taken to decorate the Nappes cascade and the lower basin of the central axis of the garden with very expensive marble sculptures. Several large groups were planned. Antoine Coysevox prepared pedestals for the models of two life-sized equestrian groups, *Fame* and *Mercury* (these formerly decorated the entry to the Tuileries gardens from the Place de la Concorde in Paris); and two enormous figure groups representing rivers by van Clève and Coustou were commissioned, along with six additional mythological groups of two or more figures.[48]

Architectural work for the king as such was for the most part kept to a minimum. However, projects were finally accepted for the new Apartment

128. Claude III Audran: design for a bath and the wall panel behind it, probably for the dauphin's house at Meudon. Coloured drawing, c. 1699

129. Workshop of Mansart: ornament for the centre of the ceiling of the King's Bedchamber at Marly (de Cotte Collection No. 1471). Drawing, 1699

130 (opposite). Pierre Denis Martin: bird's-eye view of the gardens and château of Marly (M.V. 762). Painting, 1724

of the Duke of Burgundy (first proposed in 1696), which was to be contained in a new building spanning the middle of the interior courtyard between the Grand Apartment of the Queen (then occupied by the Duchess of Burgundy) and the king's own rooms (Fig. 131).

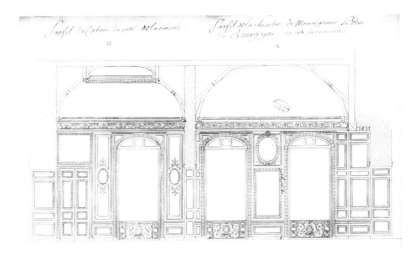

131. Elevation of the west wall of the project for the bedchamber and cabinet for the Duke of Burgundy at Versailles. Drawing, 1699

Since the king's advancing age and the state of his health suggested that for the first time his physical comfort should be considered, more efficient fireplaces were ordered for his apartments at both Versailles and Marly. These small changes were more important than they might seem, since the replacement of the fireplaces necessitated the redesigning of substantial parts of the interiors. Four new fireplaces for the central salon of Marly created a great new interior.[49]

In March 1699 Mansart's grand design for the new high altar of Notre Dame de Paris was shown to the king and approved; but the proliferation of projects eventually proved more than the treasury could afford. On 21 August Mansart recorded the fact that most projects were to be postponed until the following year.

The book in which Mansart recorded the activities for Versailles abruptly stopped on that date and resumed only the next year. The sculptures for Marly were an exception to the stoppage: Coysevox continued to be paid for the setting up of full-sized plaster models of his equestrian groups, and work on the models of the eight other groups never stopped, though payment was deferred until 1700 where possible. Furthermore, a note by Louis on Mansart's record indicates that work was to continue on the chapel until as late as 15 October; then it was to stop.

The anticipated resumption of large-scale work after the beginning of the new year (and century) never did transpire, but some projects were continued. In December of 1699 the sum of 150,000 *livres* was projected for the continuation of the chapel, and eventually slightly more than the original sum was spent. Furthermore, important works of interior architecture and the commissioning of a few paintings took place for the Apartments of the king and Madame de Maintenon at the Grand Trianon.[50] But on 11 January all the work on the great marble sculptures for Marly was postponed until 1701.

The accession to the Spanish throne of Louis's grandson Philip V in November 1700, and the inevitability of a European war against France which it brought, raised the question whether any important new projects would ever be feasible. In 1701 Louis continued some of the drastic economies which had appeared necessary the previous year. Expenditures for the chapel were reduced from a projected sum of 250,000 *livres* to a modest 73,000. Things were in slightly better shape as far as the great marble sculptures for Marly were concerned. But it would be fair to characterize the rhythm of work at Versailles as uneven, and it is clear that in spite of enthusiasm for new projects and exciting new designs, there was simply not the income to sustain activity on a level which represented even a small percentage of that which had become habitual during the 1670s and 1680s.

In spite of the financial and military problems, some work continued at Versailles. France's position as a great power in Europe had to some degree been defined in terms of her ability to support a brilliant court. It was unthinkable that the country should appear weak, whatever the financial reality. In the face of the lack of the wherewithal to move along rapidly on grand projects like the new chapel, a less costly project was found to dazzle the foreign observers of the French court. Such a project seems to have developed from a modest attempt to remodel the king's living area.

On 8 July 1701 Louis ordered that the wall between the ante-chamber adjoining his bedroom and the bedroom itself be removed, to create a new ante-chamber more than twice the size of the former room. He moved his bedroom to the room next to his former chamber, the Grand Salon, which occupied the exact centre of the suite of rooms on the west side of the marble court of the old château (see Fig. 58).

The change from Grand Salon to King's Bedroom must have seemed almost the ideal answer to the problems facing the Buildings Office at that moment. Only two changes were absolutely necessary to transform the former Salon: the construction and carving of the balustrade required by tradition for the king's bed, and the closing off of the three doorways which led from the Salon to the Hall of Mirrors. The gains from this were considerable: a new and far grander setting for the two important rituals of the king's daily life, the *levée* and *couchée*. It was certainly noticed as well that the king's chamber had come to occupy the approximate centre of the château, a change which has ever since been seen as charged with symbolic meaning.

The success of this proposal seems to have been such as to cause an important elaboration of the original project. A magnificent new fireplace was ordered on 10 July, two days after the original proposal for the chamber. By August it was decided that the east–west axis of the room needed to be slightly widened to make additional space in the area behind the balustrade. The wall between the Salon and the Hall of Mirrors was reduced in thickness to provide more space, and an ingenious and lovely design was developed to solve both structural and aesthetic needs. An ovaloid arch was made within the wall which both supported the thicker wall above and created the traditional effect of a niche for the bed, though it was only two feet deep (Fig. 132). The elegant curve of this arch has also been seen as an important step towards the development of a new light and graceful style of wall articulation. At the very least the use of white panelling with gold highlighting in the chamber represented an important break from the earlier interiors at Versailles and brought to the king's own apartment something of the lightness and charm of the decor of the collection rooms of 1692 and the zoo apartments of the Duchess of Burgundy.

A number of changes were made throughout the living and working quarters of Louis XIV at this moment, but it was the ante-chamber which was to be the most remarkable creation of this remodelling. A major problem in the planning of this large room was the lack of daylight. One pair of windows looked out on to the Cour de Marbre, while three others, far away, received some illumination from the small interior court, which had become narrower and darker because of the building of sleeping quarters for the Duke of Burgundy. The lighting problem was compounded by the decision, reached shortly after work on the Salon had begun, to raise the vault of the ceiling very high as an appropriate response to the architecture of the bedroom. It was absolutely necessary to bring more light into the room, and an oval window was added above the frieze on the wall facing the small inner court. This was the famous Bull's Eye (Fig. 133). Mirrors were also used extensively to raise the level of daytime lighting, and perhaps to demonstrate that since the French could now make large sheets of glass they were able to rival the Venetians.

But the design of the Salon of the *Œil de Bœuf* presented other serious problems. At first it had been hoped that the room could be made simply by knocking down the wall between the old ante-chamber and bedroom,

132. The bedchamber of Louis XIV. Modern model of the room as it appeared in 1702

*133. Elevation of a
project for the south wall of
the ante-chamber of the
king at Versailles with the
oval bull's-eye window.
Drawing, 1701*

leaving the pre-existing ceiling vaults connected by some kind of arch. This
proved aesthetically disastrous, because the rooms were different in their
proportions. A single vault was seen to be a necessity. An uninterrupted
curve rising to a sufficiently grand height was quite impossible in this area,
since the former bedroom was located under the slanting slate roof of the
old château of Louis XIII.

The ceiling (Fig. 134) now rises in two stages of vaulting. One runs all
the way around the room at approximately the level of the famous oval
window (and of the pendant window element of similar shape filled with
mirrors on the opposite side of the room). Then there is a second small
cornice, from which the ceiling vault actually springs. This vaulting system
just manages to fit under the slope of the roof at the north-east end.

Those responsible for the decorative details were brilliantly successful in
avoiding any trace of an awkward transition between the two levels of the
vaulting. They added a graceful relief of playing children (Fig. 135); the

134. The Salon of the Œil de Bœuf (ante-chamber to the king's bedroom), 1702. Versailles

135. Lespagnaudelle and others: the frieze of the playing children. Relief sculpture in plaster, 1702. Versailles, Salon of the Œil de Bœuf

newly fashionable white and gold colour scheme was again used, and the gilding of the trellis-like background pattern behind the frolicking children brought a special sparkle to the room.

The whole remodelling was managed with both economy and speed. Much was left unchanged beyond a paint job. The pilasters and the frieze of medals and garlands of the old royal bedroom were preserved. One doorway still contains elements of the arms of Marie-Thérèse, who had died in 1683. It must also have been left completely untouched.

No time was wasted. By October 1701 the furnishings for the new bedroom began to arrive. In the matter of a few months a breathtaking new decor had been created, and this precisely at the time when a Grand Alliance between the maritime powers and the Emperor Leopold I was being formed.

The project of the completion of the new chapel and the rooms connected with it, on the other hand, ran into very serious difficulties. Within a short time its completion became a matter of considerable controversy. Madame de Maintenon – for the first time – took a stand strongly opposed to the king on an important issue of state. According to Mademoiselle d'Aumale, 'she did everything that she possibly could to oppose the magnificent chapel which the king was having built at Versailles, because of the wretched state of the people at the time and because she believed that soon Versailles would no longer be the seat of the court.' (She must have believed a permanent move to Marly would take place.) Louis seems to have seen the completion of the chapel as a very important political act and to have scraped together the money to continue, though he often had to resort to dubious practices of deferring payments to his masons and artists.

The initial impact of the war over the Spanish succession was particularly hard on the chapel. 1702 was a terrible year. Of the hundred thousand *livres* projected, less than ten thousand seem to have been spent. Nor do the years 1703, 1704 and 1705 appear to have been much better. In spite of the meagre sums available for the chapel, the sculptors began to receive payments in 1704 for decorations associated with the area of the roof, such as the carving of gargoyles for the drains and the column capitals of the Premier Étage.

For a time the fate of the chapel was certainly in some doubt. The Duke of Marlborough and Prince Eugene of Savoy had begun to win some of their legendary victories, such as the Battle of Blenheim (Blindheim) on 13 August 1704. In 1706 Louis wrote to his grandson, the King of Spain, that the outcome of military events was in the hands of God; 'we must await with submission whatever He wishes to do for the good of Europe.' The almost medieval tone of this statement would appear to go well with a programme of church building, and it was around 1706 that work on the chapel resumed on a much larger scale, particularly on the painted and sculptural decorations. During some of the darkest days of French history, between 1706 and 1710, artists were steadily at work creating a brilliant and sumptuous building to the glory of God. The chapel which rose high above Louis's palace seems in some way to testify to a new role for the divine in the governance of France. The new building significantly altered the message of largely secular power conveyed by Versailles before its construction.

In its broad lines the new chapel followed the designs of the chapel made twelve years earlier in the time of Louvois (see p. 150). Two great monuments which related the royal traditions of France and the church seem to have been fused to create the plan of the earlier project (Fig. 136). The general shape of both the ground plan and the exterior elevation of the chapel were designed like the Sainte Chapelle, the great palace chapel of the french king Saint Louis on the Île de la Cité in Paris. The Emperor Charlemagne's Palatine Chapel at Aix-la-Chapelle (Aachen) also had a fundamental influence on the Versailles design. Charlemagne's chapel suggested

136. Elevation of the south side of a project for the chapel of the château of Versailles. Coloured drawing, 1687(?)

the idea of a church with an important upstairs floor, a tribune for the king; and the Versailles design shares with the Aix chapel an arcaded ground floor, with a colonnade above. The Versailles chapel is dedicated to Saint Louis.

When Mansart began again in 1699, the new projects, if anything, made the medieval sources more obvious still. But a drawing of an elevation of the chapel, now in Stockholm (Fig. 137), introduces two further important changes. First, the tribune floor has been made higher and is consequently

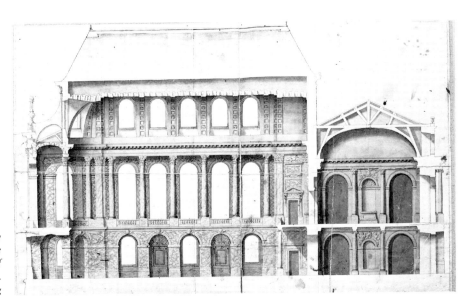

137. Elevation of the south side of a project for the chapel of the château of Versailles (T.H.C. 8067). Coloured drawing

emphasized more than on the earlier plan (Fig. 136), and the pilasters which had been substituted for Charlemagne's columns have here been more correctly rendered as columns. Secondly, changes of proportions stressed the comparison with Saint Louis's Sainte Chapelle. The new design increased both the height and the verticality of the whole in a manner which suggests a response to the soaring qualities of Gothic architecture. This was also reflected in the exterior elevation of the building: the roof-line was changed and a steep slope and much higher roof were created (Fig. 137).

Further changes beyond those seen in Fig. 137 were made in the design of the chapel before it was finally constructed. Dangeau informs us that in March 1699 Louis decided to reject the idea of finishing the interior with coloured marbles (these are clearly shown in Fig. 137) and to use ordinary stone. This was for reasons of the king's health, in the hope that a stone other than marble would produce a less damp interior. An entirely new approach to the decoration was developed. The white stone walls were enriched with ornament and other relief sculptures. The element of colour was to be added by a vast painted ceiling, not included in any of the early plans, and by the use of brightly coloured marble on the ground floor (Fig. 138).

Although the use of uncoloured stone appears at first to be a move towards the simplicity of a more classical style, it seems quite possible that the designers of the chapel attempted to convey in the interior decor (Fig. 139) something of the shimmering brilliance of the Sainte Chapelle, famed for the effect of its marvellous, almost weightless, glittering walls of stained glass. The large windows of the new tribune designs brought in a great deal of light, which played on columns and the low stone reliefs of the interior walls to reduce somewhat the potentially weighty effect of the stone, while the gilt and the intense colours of the upper vault gave some approximation of the dazzling effect and colour of Saint Louis's chapel.

The Versailles chapel was, however, something more than an imitation of the Gothic. A sensibility to the differences in the idea of mystical revelation between the cultures of the Middle Ages and the time of Louis XIV seems also to have been rather subtly expressed. The clear white light of the Age of Reason replaces the more mysterious ambience created by the rich reds and blues of Gothic stained glass.

It has always been said (and frequently lamented) that the influence of the Italian baroque style reached unprecedented heights here, particularly in the decorative richness of the finished exterior (Fig. 140) and the Berninesque style of the many statues of the Apostles, Evangelists, Doctors of the Church, and saints and allegorical figures of Christian virtues which stood on the exterior balustrade above the frieze on top of the tribune floor. No

138. *Ground plan showing the design of the flooring of the chapel of the château of Versailles.*
Coloured drawing, c. 1700

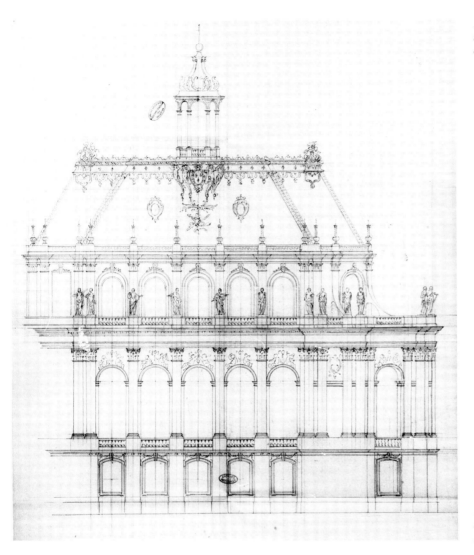

139 (opposite). *Interior of the royal chapel of the château of Versailles*

140. *Elevation of the south side of the Versailles chapel. Drawing, after 1706*

less related to the artistic traditions of the Italian world of Bernini was a remarkably innovative feature of the great ceiling. In the very centre (Fig. 141) the illusionistic architecture (which was rendered in the ornamental style of the walls, but in gilt) was broken through to show the Heavenly Host in the clouds, with God the Father looking down. The end sections of the ceiling – that is, the areas over the altar and the tribune – were also rendered so as to suggest the illusion of an opening into celestial space (Fig. 142). This Italianism was not, however, just an attempt to evoke great

Italian models (such as the Gesù in Rome) but, at least in concept, was consistent with Mansart's attempt to create some equivalent to the sense of saturation of light suggested by the stained glass of the Gothic interiors, giving an entirely new meaning to the style.

The existence of three different versions of the programme of subjects represented in the paintings leaves no doubt that trouble was taken with the choice of figures and narrative subjects to convey a definite message to the visitor or worshipper. Unfortunately, no contemporary explanation of the programme has survived, and no one has yet explained the meaning, but at the most basic level it is certainly closely connected with the functions of the various parts of the church.[51]

The three spectacular breakthroughs into the heavens in the middle and ends of the ceiling contain the three parts of the Trinity: Father, Son and Holy Spirit. The Ascension of Christ is shown over the altar, where His body and blood were believed to be present in the celebration of the mass.

141 (opposite). *Antoine Coypel:* God the Father in Paradise, *with figures of Old Testament prophets and other scenes in feigned relief. Central ceiling painting, 1709–10. Versailles, chapel*

142. *Jean Jouvenet:* The Descent of the Holy Spirit *and above it, in feigned relief,* The Emperor Charlemagne *(by A. Coypel). Painted ceiling, 1709–10. Versailles, chapel*

At the other end of the ceiling, by the tribune, the Holy Spirit is present in a scene representing the Pentecost; thus the king was associated with divine revelation to man and the spread of the faith on earth. God the Father was shown in the centre of the entire ceiling. Near this part of the Trinity,

143. Antoine Coypel:
study for an Old Testament
prophet for the ceiling of
the chapel of Versailles
(Inv. 25825 bis).
Drawing, c. 1709

associated with the Old Testament, eight of the prophets (Fig. 143) were shown seated in front of the illusionistic architecture. There are inscriptions quoting their sayings. Here an exact sense of the message of the ceiling is particularly difficult to grasp, but there seem to be a number of references to kingship and to the restoration and preservation by the kings of Israel of the temple of Jerusalem (Daniel 9:24), which would be appropriate for the splendid chapel of Louis XIV.

The painted programme of the ceiling confirms the connection of the building to the great architectural prototypes mentioned above, the chapel of Aix and the Sainte Chapelle, since a feigned relief in the illusionistic painting of the architecture of the ceiling near the tribune shows Charlemagne (Fig. 142), while another in a symmetrical position at the altar end shows Saint Louis in prayer.

What emerged from the decision to enrich the simple white stone walls of the interior was a whole new repertory of ornamental designs, uniquely delightful and rather unexpected in a holy place, exuding the charm and grace which had become a recent part of the tradition of design at Versailles. The architectural framework for this decorative display was kept simple, while the ornament spread over wide areas. The designs kept large objects to a minimum and used a massing of intricate shapes and forms to create a lace-like effect. The originality and delicacy of this style can perhaps be suggested by looking at the manner in which the ornamental designers rendered a traditionally grand form. A series of religious trophies was designed to decorate the piers on the ground floor of the chapel (Fig. 144). The idea of trophies filling long vertical rectangular panels had been used extensively at Versailles earlier, particularly in the Hall of Mirrors and the adjoining Salons of War and Peace (Fig. 66). The motif was particularly in mind at the time of the construction of the chapel, since certain of these trophy groups in the palace had been cast in bronze and gilded after 1700. The chapel reliefs resemble the trophies of the Hall of Mirrors etc. in showing a group of highly ornamental objects entwined with ribbons and garlands. The difference lies in the apparent weight of the objects shown. Certain of the chapel reliefs become predominantly confections of flowers, branches and ribbons (Fig. 145). The chapel designers reach their original best in the extraordinary round ceiling ornaments of the semi-domes of the side aisles (Fig. 146).

This ornament does not come from the traditions of masonry and stone carving, but is a translation into the medium of stone of the delicate ornament found slightly earlier in the panelling and plasterwork of the apartments of the zoo, the renovated apartment of the king at Versailles, and also of a new bedroom for the king at the Grand Trianon (after 1703).

The furnishings of the chapel were no less fine than the architecture as a whole. A lively drawing of a project for a confessional showing the ornamental scheme (Fig. 147) suggests that an interesting blending of the ornamental styles of Bérain and the Mansart workshop was taking place.

144. *Attributed to René Charpentier:* Grace, *a trophy representing the Holy Spirit and baptism* (The Baptism of Christ?) *for the chapel of Versailles* (T.H.C. 1004). *Drawing, inscribed 'Charpentier',* c. 1708

145. Chandelier and garlands, bottom portion of a trophy decorating a pier of the ambulatory. Relief sculpture, c. 1708. Versailles, chapel

146 (opposite). View of the south aisle of the ground floor of the chapel. Versailles

147. Study for a confessional for the chapel of Versailles. Drawing, c. 1709–10

One decorative element in particular needs to be mentioned because it is seen as possibly the first example of the Rococo style in France. 'It is the organ case, executed in 1709–10 and still surviving [Fig. 148], which most fully embodies the new spirit appearing in the decoration of the chapel ... In the Organ of Versailles ... there is no effort to disguise the plate faces by treatment *à l'Italienne*. The pipes are supported by a spreading cove in a manner unused since the sixteenth century ... The case for the first time takes on a concave form, to remain characteristic throughout the following reign ...'[52] The morphic twist on the palm trunks rising at the angles was also a striking innovation in furniture design.

The building of the chapel necessitated the construction of two large vestibules between the garden façade of the north wing and the New Building, on top of each other, giving access both to the royal tribune on the Premier Étage and to the ground-floor level of the church (Fig. 149). These

148 (opposite). *Attributed to Pierre Le Pautre: organ case. Carved wood, 1709– 10. Versailles, tribune of the chapel above the altar*

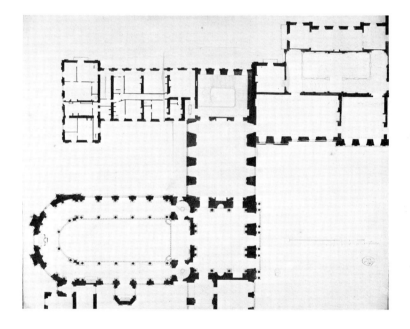

149. *Plan of the chapel, its vestibule and the new salon connecting the chapel with the Grand Apartment at Versailles. Drawing, c. 1711*

were executed in the yellowish-white native stone of the exterior, and, though rather simpler than the chapel itself in ornament, were nonetheless of a similarly refined design, with something of the same elegance.

Little was done besides the chapel at Versailles during the long period of its construction, but a few significant changes were made in the gardens, primarily in the *bosquets*. The Water Gallery was replaced by the rather dull 'Room of the Chestnut Trees', a simple affair where a few ancient portrait busts were interspersed among stone benches in the opening in the woods formerly occupied by the *Galerie des Antiquités*. This downgrading was symptomatic of the time.

But a delightful final touch – the charming, if a trifle awkward, Children's Island (Fig. 150) – was completed. This playful and joyous work renders in plastic form the spirit of so much of the decorative art of the era. It has been rightly compared to the relief of the playing children in the frieze of the Salon of the *Œil de Bœuf* (see Fig. 135).

The great Mansart died suddenly in 1708, but the brilliant style of his late period was preserved by Robert de Cotte, his successor as first architect. However, the return to a more traditional superintendency under the Duke d'Antin must have created an atmosphere very different from that in 1699 when Mansart's appointment represented a triumphal moment in a great career. The idea of further great works receded rapidly, and the very last years of Louis's Versailles saw only the completion of the last Mansart projects and works which really must be considered maintenance.

150. Jean Hardy: the Children's Island. Lead sculpture, 1710. Versailles, gardens

CONCLUSION

151. Nicodemus Tessin the younger: exterior elevation of the pavilion of Apollo for Versailles (T.H.C. 1199)

The two last monumental projects of the reign of Louis XIV were not made by the king's great designers at all but by the Swedish royal architect, Nicodemus Tessin the Younger. A pavilion of Apollo was planned for the end of the Grand Canal (of Versailles) or for the Satory hillside above the Swiss pool to the south of the château (Fig. 151), and, somewhat surprisingly at this late date, a vast project for the completion of the Louvre was once again presented to the old king.

Tessin's admiration for Louis was almost boundless. In a letter written, not for the French, but to his own man in Paris, he said the following concerning a visit to Paris by his son: 'I dare say that one of the most important reasons for sending him to France is to allow him the good fortune to see a king to whom the past as well as the future will hardly furnish an example of similar wisdom and grandeur.' Under these circumstances Tessin's gestures of homage are hardly surprising.

Tessin had several motives for designing these works. The drawings and the plans of both the projects were brought to Paris by his own son. 'I hope that they will only be presented [to the king] at a very favourable moment, and will be able to gain for my son an opportunity so that he will be tolerated by the court somewhat better than a foreigner, whom they look upon with complete indifference.' This fact certainly accounts for the date of their presentation. But the selection of the projects and their meaning have little to do with the son's visit. They provide instead an interesting insight into what was perceived to be the situation of the arts at the time in France by an exceptionally well-informed foreigner, one who had kept a personal artistic representative, Cronström, in Paris since 1693.

Tessin felt that the death of Mansart in 1708 had made an important difference; the group around the superintendent was no longer all-powerful, and outside input might be tolerated. Of his own plans Tessin remarks: 'I hope that they will be to the taste of the court; at least the deceased jealousy of Mr Mansart will no longer be directly opposed to them and M. the Duke d'Antin should be above being confused by false criticism.' It is not quite clear whether Tessin thought the age of genius had come to an end in France.

The most important message of Tessin's gesture is certainly that he had no doubt that the standards of French design had reached a point of universal applicability. His plans for the Louvre, which he had worked on for some years and which he had presented to the king in 1706, suggest further that he thought the principles of French design were well enough understood (even abroad) for foreigners to begin to compete on French ground. Tessin's correspondence with Cronström indicates that he was familiar with Mansart's ideas of the problems presented by the completion of work on the Louvre, that he had reflected upon them and believed that his solution was both workable on those terms and the best yet proposed. But the awe in which he held the French achievements of the time was nonetheless considerable. Despite the success of his own major works for the kings of Sweden and Denmark, Tessin was clearly impressed by the high standards of judgement of a great number of fine connoisseurs of architecture in France. He worried about their criticism of his plans. He was even moved to write (on 19 January 1715): 'A foreigner who makes an appropriate gesture for the Glory of the King should merit a bit more than the ordinary indulgence'.

Tessin's views on the strengths of French design, expressed when he spoke of the areas of importance for his son, who was in Paris on an educational tour, are most interesting. 'I would be absolutely delighted if he would apply himself [to the study of] the interior decoration of buildings as well as to gardening, because it is in these areas that they excel in France ...' (18 June 1715). Earlier, on 14 July 1714, Tessin had written: 'According to my advice he should learn to imitate interior decoration and the comfort and convenience of the French, while in exteriors the example of Italy should be supreme.' Tessin's francophilia is perhaps incompletely suggested in this second statement. In his letters it is clear that the use of the word Italy implies not just contemporary Italian architecture but also the surviving monuments of ancient Rome. When political factors suddenly permitted, the first part of Tessin's son's trip abroad was switched from Italy to Paris, and a long stay of fifteen months was contemplated.

Tessin's Pavilion of Apollo was quite clearly intended as the homage of an important architect to a king who had been instrumental in bringing the art of architecture to one of the brilliant climaxes in its whole history. The flattery began with the presumption that, if it were worthy, the king would actually build a structure whose message was the glorification of Louis and of his reign by the creation of a thing of beauty. Tessin's scheme was an entirely suitable one in terms of the architectural and artistic ideals of the time. The building sprang from a complex, ingenious, and politically meaningful concept which blended a number of important ideas relating to both the greatness of the king and the ideals of architecture.

The name of the building suggested the entire programme: Apollo as the device of the king and Apollo as the patron of the muses. Though ostensibly a garden pavilion, Tessin's building took a form reminiscent of Roman temple architecture, the great centralized Christian temples of the Italian Renaissance, and also of the great Italian villas of Palladio, all high art. The most surprising aspect of the structure was its lack of windows in the walls and, significantly, the use of mirrors on the interior. Tessin's idea of Italy for exteriors, France for interiors, is immediately apparent here. But the message of his building was far from being this simple.

The explanation he gave of one aspect of his work, the lighting of the interior from the dome above, suggests that the building as a whole had a very complex meaning:

With regard to the Salon of Apollo, it may be called whatever seems to fit the occasion, but since the sun is at its greatest strength when it is highest in the sky, it would seem that light from above is preferable to any other kind in relation to the sun [and in this room] is to be found right in the middle of the vault. This light which comes from above is that which is esteemed in Italy more than all other kinds and is used to embellish all kinds of things. At the Rotunda [the Pantheon] in Rome one notices that every detail is enhanced by the strength of the light from above, and since there is nowhere in the world where novelty is more appreciated than in Paris, I am sure that if a salon of this type could actually be constructed the effect of it would surpass what many could imagine.

In the area of the arts, Louis's most bitter enemies and antagonistic critics willingly accepted the standards of elegance and good taste of the court of France. Prince William of Orange, whose political and military career in Holland and later in England (where he became William III in 1688) was largely built around opposition to Louis – both politically and militarily – unhesitatingly seized the opportunity to employ an important French architect, interior decorator and furniture designer, Daniel Marot, when the possibility presented itself. Marot, who had worked as an engraver for Jean Bérain and was a Huguenot, fled from France after the revocation of the Edict of Nantes in 1685. He was in William's employ by 1687 at the latest, became his interior architect, and was even taken to England after William came to the English throne. He worked at Hampton Court and Kensington in 1695. Furthermore, in 1696–8 Marot gave Louis's bitterest political enemies, the Dutch States General, an audience hall in an adaptation of the French taste (the Binnenhof at The Hague). He planned De Voorst, the Dutch country house of William's favourite, the Earl of Albemarle, and designed splendid furnishings for William's favourite home, Het Loo at Apeldoorn (see Fig. 80).

Het Loo has been called a 'Dutch Versailles', a claim which the modest size and private character of the place can hardly support, but Marot's work there shows clearly that William must have been in basic agreement with Tessin about the superiority of things French in matters of interior design, comfort and garden design.

The grander message of political power suggested by the vast size and brilliant life-style of Versailles was also emulated by Louis's enemies. In 1693, the pre-eminent royal figure of the League of Augsburg, the Emperor Leopold, had plans drawn up by J. B. Fischer von Erlach for a great palace, Schönbrunn, in the country outside Vienna at the site of a hunting lodge destroyed during the siege of Vienna by the Turks (1683). The engraving of a project for the palace by Fischer (Fig. 152) leaves no doubt that rivalling Versailles was the idea, though an anti-French attitude may have been expressed by the use of a design similar to the one made for the Louvre by the Italian Bernini. Schönbrunn was begun in 1696, towards the end of the League War. The date suggests an arrogant gesture in the face of the misery of France at the time. Views of the palace as built, with its regular yellow façade rising behind straight *allées* in the geometric patterning of a French-

*152. J. B. Fischer von
Erlach: ideal design for
Schönbrunn (near Vienna).
Engraving, design
from c. 1693*

style garden, seem Versaillesque; but Schönbrunn is not nearly as large as Versailles, nor were its appendages and gardens so vast or elaborate.

Perhaps a more successful Viennese confrontation of the grandeur of the life-style of the French king is the suburban residence of a foreign prince, another of Louis's military enemies, Prince Eugene of Savoy, who was the difficult father of Louis's favourite, the Duchess of Burgundy. He began by developing a hillside garden with a fine view of Vienna to the east of the Palais Mansfled-Fondi, which he also owned. Work had started relatively modestly with terracing, and continued in 1714–16 with the construction at the foot of the hill of a curious building which was a mixture of suburban villa and orangery. Some of the interiors of this structure, now called the Lower Belvedere, are notable for their French taste.

It was in 1721–2, however, that Prince Eugene made his most significant gesture. He commissioned Lukas von Hildebrandt to build him another structure, the Upper Belvedere (Fig. 153), which was strikingly palatial in its appearance, certainly a rival to Schönbrunn. But the wonder of it, which might even have impressed the then deceased Louis XIV, was that it was only a garden pavilion, though of truly staggering size. Furthermore, with this work Eugene was able to leave a permanent monument to his own military importance to the Empire, one which became, and still is, one of the great sights of the former imperial capital.

One monument was actually built with the intention of belittling Louis's

153. Lukas von Hildebrandt: the Upper Belvedere, Vienna, seen from below on the garden side

154. John Vanbrugh and
Nicholas Hawksmoor:
Blenheim Palace,
Oxfordshire, the north
front. 1705–16

contribution to the arts. This was called Blenheim Palace, offered by a grateful Queen Anne and the English parliament to the general John Churchill, Duke of Marlborough, in honour of his great military victory near Blindheim in 1704 (Fig. 154).

A number of factors seem to have led to the construction of this vastly outsized British country house. One was the Duchess of Marlborough's close friendship with the queen, which prompted her to give the Churchills the royal estate of Woodstock Park. But the genesis of the new building, which replaced a famous old house (pulled down by the duchess), had much to do with the state of architecture in England at the time. The many triumphs of Wren were standing or moving towards completion, and it seemed that a promising younger generation of architects was reaching maturity. Blenheim was surely intended to show that British architecture was entering a great period.

Ideological considerations seem to have been fundamental. It was no coincidence that Sir John Vanbrugh, an officer and playwright, was selected as the architect of Blenheim. He had expressed the view that greater architecture could be built under a constitutional monarchy and Whig liberty than under an absolutist French king. Another motive behind the building of Blenheim was apparently to show the French king that a grateful English nation could do for one of its generals what the French nation could do only for its king. This idea appears to have particularly appealed to Queen Anne.

Under these circumstances, it is somewhat surprising that the design by Vanbrugh, who worked as a team with Nicholas Hawksmoor, is not in any real sense anti-French. Most historians are agreed that much of Blenheim comes ultimately from seventeenth-century French architecture. Certainly the original garden setting of the palace (destroyed in the eighteenth century by Capability Brown) was thought to be in the French style, and the ornament throughout, particularly on the earlier parts of the interior, seems to have been largely French-inspired. It appears that the Blenheim designers, like Tessin, did Louis XIV's Buildings Office the homage of accepting much of what was developed there.

✻

It has often been said that after Versailles every prince in Europe sought to imitate the residence of Louis XIV. No one ever wanted one just like it, and nothing like it was ever attempted until Herrenchiemsee was built by an eccentric Bavarian king nearly two centuries later.

Versailles, instead, represented to contemporaries a source of good ideas; it was admired for the high level of design exemplified throughout. Versailles meant much more than the actual buildings and park which the Persian ambassador saw in 1715. It was a place where the art of design had reached a level that set most of the standards and principles of good design for the whole era. That is why the Swedish crown kept a full-time representative – at ambassadorial level – in Paris from 1693 to 1718, whose job it was to follow the arts in France for the Swedish royal architect. It also seems possible that other powers of the time would have done the same if their political relations with the French crown had been better. Cronström's stay in Paris is a clear indication of the coming of age of French art and represents the achievement of a goal which had long preoccupied the builders of Versailles, the creation by the French king of a new Rome, a European art capital which, like Rome earlier in the century, could become the training ground in the arts for the whole of Europe.

A GENERAL NOTE ON
BIBLIOGRAPHY

Anthony Blunt wrote in the *Pelican History of Art* in 1953 that the story of Versailles had mostly been told. He was referring to the documentary history by Pierre de Nolhac, the famous Conservateur-en-Chef of the Musée which was housed in the château of Versailles. Nolhac began in the last years of the nineteenth century to correct the faulty mythological history of Versailles which had developed in guide books; he carefully surveyed an enormous quantity of surviving written documents and drawings, a task greatly simplified by the completion a few years before by Jules Guiffrey of the publication of the payments of the *Maison du Roi* during the reign of Louis XIV (five giant volumes known today as the *Comptes des Bâtiments du Roi*). Nolhac's first book, *La Création de Versailles* (Paris, 1901), has rightly been acclaimed as a magisterial study, one unsurpassed to this day in its solid and clear narrative presentation, the clever solutions it offered to a remarkable number of difficult problems, and its ingenuity in bridging the *lacunae* of our knowledge with convincing hypotheses. Even Nolhac's footnotes are a mine of knowledge and still should not be overlooked.

During the years after the publication of the *Création* Nolhac continued his researches and produced an astonishing number of ground-breaking articles and popular books on various topics which added to the knowledge of Versailles after about 1670, where the narration of the *Création* had stopped.

Fortunately for the student of Versailles, Nolhac also produced a second major volume continuing his narrative of the history of Versailles up to the death of Louis XIV in 1715, *Versailles Résidence de Louis XIV* (Paris, 1925). This book, which must have been under way for a very long time, was perhaps less thorough than Nolhac's first great work and lacks illustrations, but is still a rich mine of information, particularly valuable for its extensive citation of important source material, much of it otherwise difficult of access.

Nolhac continued his history of Versailles with two later works, *Ver-*

sailles au XVIII siècle (Paris, 1926) and *Trianon* (Paris, 1927), but neither of these books, useful as they are, reveals the exhaustive study which had been the awesome characteristic of the *Création*. However, they did contribute to the impression that the history of Versailles had been written, in spite of the fact that refinements to Nolhac's ideas would be made, notably by Alfred Marie and Fiske Kimball.

Kimball contributed to the knowledge of the history of the interior architecture of the château and the Grand Trianon, most notably in his book *The Creation of the Rococo* (Philadelphia, 1943). But it was Marie, with his colleague at the Bibliothèque Nationale, R. A. Weigert, and Pierre Francastel, who made the discovery which most dated Nolhac's work.

Word had been out for some time that important drawings for Versailles existed at the Nationalmuseum in Stockholm. Ragnar Josephson, beginning in the 1920s, published some remarkable discoveries, most notably the drawings by Le Nôtre of the Grand Trianon commissioned by the Swedish court architect Nicodemus Tessin in 1694. Other articles by Josephson brought to light the existence in Stockholm of a description of Versailles written by Tessin during a trip to France in 1687, obviously a very important source since most descriptions of Versailles were notoriously lacking in details about the architecture and decoration. In 1926 Josephson and Pierre Francastel published important excerpts from Tessin's description (*Revue de l'histoire de Versailles . . .*, No. 28). While Francastel went on to publish the first study of the great sculptural projects for Versailles (*La Sculpture de Versailles*, Paris, 1930), few scholars beyond Josephson knew that the Tessin collection actually consisted of some 10,000 drawings, that the correspondence concerning their acquisition had survived with them, and that the eighteenth-century court architect Cronstedt had acquired nearly 10,000 more, including many drawings bought from the estate after the death of Claude III Audran, the last member of a whole dynasty of artists who had worked for Louis XIV.

During the Second World War the Swedes mounted two important exhibitions which began to give a better idea of the Stockholm holdings, but they were largely unknown to the rest of the world.

Later Marie and Weigert began studying the Stockholm material, and many sensational discoveries were the immediate result. A few of these were published in articles or in Weigert's works, but they revealed only the tip of the iceberg, and the importance of the Stockholm material was not generally recognized until a large selection of the drawings was exhibited at the Bibliothèque Nationale in Paris in 1950 and at Versailles in 1951.

The newly discovered Stockholm material shed light on many obscure areas of the history of Versailles; in contrast, an enormous book by

A. Laprade on François d'Orbay (Paris, 1960) muddied the waters with a series of attributions to this important architectural draughtsman which wrongly made of him the greatest French architect of the period 1660–80. The book contains important documentation not available elsewhere, but Laprade's paranoid fantasy that d'Orbay had done the work but received none of the recognition resulted in the attribution to him of important Versailles projects. Actually it is very difficult to understand d'Orbay's role at Versailles. He very obviously made drawings of the projects of other architects, and much remains to be clarified in the area of attributional studies of the drawings of Versailles. Subsequent writers such as Marie have avoided these difficult problems by giving double attributions, e.g. 'Le Vau/d'Orbay', which simply skirts the question.

An important scholarly event which made possible the systematic study of the Stockholm material took place in 1964, when Weigert, with Carl Hernmarck of the Nationalmuseum, published the Tessin correspondence related to the drawings (*Les Relations Artistiques entre la France et la Suède 1693–1718, correspondence, (extraits) Nicodème Tessin le jeune et Daniel Cronström*, Stockholm), though their failure to illustrate the book reduces its usefulness.

At the same time Marie was preparing a study in four parts which was intended to update Nolhac, specifically by publishing a considerable body of material either overlooked by Nolhac or unknown to him, including many drawings from Stockholm and many more at the Bibliothèque Nationale in Paris, where Marie had worked for years. Marie's books also included many early engravings. His *Naissance de Versailles* (2 vols., Paris, 1968), *Mansart à Versailles* (2 vols., Paris, 1972), and *Versailles au Temps de Louis XIV* (Paris, 1976), have transformed the study of Versailles, perhaps doubling the visual source material available to the student.

The *Versailles* (Paris, 1961; reissued 1985) of Pierre Verlet, the great historian of eighteenth-century French furniture, managed for the first time to give some sense of this vast subject within the scope of a single volume. Verlet's book is full of fascinating facts, but unfortunately the usefulness of his text was limited by the surprising origins of his work and by an editor who refused to provide illustrations. The book began as a series of lectures delivered while the author was in prison camp during the Second World War. It was apparently for that reason that Verlet provided no notes, a fact that is particularly regrettable since he is a famous student of the archives. The notorious document cited by Verlet but untraceable subsequently by other scholars has become a kind of professional nightmare of Versailles studies.

At the present time specialized studies in various areas of the arts under

Louis XIV are adding considerably to the Versailles material. Certain mini-monographs in the form of articles have appeared, such as Liliane Lange on the Grotto of Thetis (*Art de France*, I, 1961) and Gérard Mabille on the Ménagerie (*Gazette des Beaux Arts*, 1974); Simone Hoog's study of the Labyrinthe should soon appear. Specialized works outside architectural history have also been published. To give just a few examples, Antoine Schnapper was able to discover much of the history of and even many of the paintings for the Grand Trianon (*Tableaux pour le Trianon de marbre 1688-1714*, Paris, 1967) while the study of the sculpture of Versailles, free-standing, relief, and even ornament, has advanced enormously in the illustrated revision of Lami undertaken by François Souchal (*French Sculptors of the 17th and 18th Centuries, The Reign of Louis XIV*, Oxford, 1977). Robert Berger, in a careful reading of the documents and drawings for Versailles of 1668-9 (*Architectura*, Vol. 10, 1980), has convincingly reconstructed the complicated history of the château during that pivotal period.

Other new facts have emerged from monographic studies such as Schnapper's *Jean Jouvenet* (Paris, 1974), Thomas Hedin's book on the Marsy brothers (Columbia, Missouri, 1983), F. Hamilton Hazlehurst's *Gardens of Illusion ... Le Nostre* (Nashville, Tennessee, 1980), and Margaret Stuffman's *Charles de la Fosse* (*Gazette des Beaux Arts*, 1964). Archaeological and related documentary studies of the château itself, such as those of Christian Baulez, have also contributed important new material.

Thus it may now just begin to be possible to say, as Blunt mistakenly did in 1953, that the story has mostly been told. Some would even add that it has been told in minute and ultimately frustrating detail. Yet very little has appeared which tries to explain the meaning of what was built at Versailles. Exploration of the intended symbolic meaning of Versailles is in its infancy. Louis Hautecœur's study *Louis XIV, Roi-Soleil* (Paris, 1953), brief as it is, has found no successor. And, perhaps most surprisingly, art historians have left it to the historians to make a half-hearted job of explaining why things were done as they were. An interpretive literature on Versailles is largely lacking, particularly one that builds carefully on the well-documented facts. Fiske Kimball's remarks on the creative personalities of interior decoration and their manner of working at Versailles set a standard which too few have sought to emulate.

Possibly a new era of Versailles studies is in the offing. Certainly this generation of art historians is keenly aware of the importance of the circumstances of patronage in the creation of works of art. Bertrand Jestaz's precocious study of the Grand Trianon (*Gazette des Beaux Arts*, 1964) asked for the first time fundamental questions about its curious plan. Before him no one had even wondered what Trianon was supposed to represent.

He also raised crucial questions about the role of Louis XIV as a designer as well as patron. Gerold Weber's study of French fountains during the reign of Louis XIV (including Versailles; 1985) developed interesting and convincing ideas about the effects, many of them positive, of the forced collaboration between the major artists of the era.

The publication by Danielle Gallet-Guerne and Christian Baulez of *Versailles, Dessins d'architecture de la Direction Générale des Bâtiments du Roi* (Paris, 1983), provides a fundamental reference work and will certainly lead to many interesting discoveries. This description of over 3,000 drawings at the Archives Nationales is well indexed by topography, by the names of persons on all the sheets and by types of architecture. Unfortunately it is sparsely illustrated, but the descriptions are full enough to aid in the discovery of drawings related to various projects.

NOTE ON THE LOCATIONS OF MANY ELEVATIONS, PLANS AND EARLY VIEWS OF VERSAILLES

When Charles Le Brun died in 1690, Louis XIV took possession of the contents of his studio, including thousands of drawings. The drawing collection has remained largely intact and is housed today at the Cabinet des Dessins of the Louvre. In addition to the many detailed studies for the painted and sculpted decor of Versailles, a more limited number of plans and elevations undoubtedly originating from the King's Buildings Office found their way into the Le Brun collection. Illustrations of most of this collection have been published in the Guiffrey–Marcel catalogue of the Louvre drawings, French School, under the name of Le Brun. An updated version of the G.M. catalogue is now nearing completion. A very few extra-large drawings from Le Brun's collection are stored at Versailles and the Louvre.

A large number of drawings, presumably from the King's Buildings Office, passed into the collection of Jules Hardouin-Mansart and from him to his successor as chief architect, Robert de Cotte. This de Cotte collection was transferred largely intact into the collections of the Cabinet des Estampes of the Paris Bibliothèque Nationale, where these sheets may be recognized by their four-digit inventory numbers. Unfortunately they were dispersed throughout the many albums of the topographical collection of the Cabinet during the nineteenth century, though they are readily retrievable by means of a manuscript card index kept at the Cabinet which was compiled by Alfred Marie half a century ago. A single highly important album of this de Cotte collection found its way to the Bibliothèque de l'Institut, where it remains today.

Of comparable importance to the two collections mentioned above are the enormous holdings of the French Archives Nationales. The principal element of this collection is the famous o¹ series, which contains the remaining material related to the royal household (Maison du Roi). This material was organized during the eighteenth century by the architects of the king's household, with the drawings and plans being filed according to the part of the château or park for which they were made. Although material from the reigns of Louis XV and XVI is predominant, a considerable number of earlier documents appear to have been saved and filed with the later material for historical and more practical use (for example in restoration). (See Madame Gallet's index of these drawings, Archives Nationales, Paris, 1983.)

The hundreds of drawings and plans collected by Nicodemus Tessin the younger and his successor, Carl Hårleman, are preserved in the National-museum in Stockholm. A useful guide to them is the volume of correspondence related to their acquisition (see p. 222 above). The drawings are numbered and have been completely photographed; a volume of reduced-size photos kept at the Nationalmuseum greatly facilitates the study of this material, though the collection is only partly catalogued and no project for its integral publication seems to be under way. The publication of Tessin's travel notes and sketches, which form an important element of this collection, does not appear to be in prospect at the moment.

Cronstedt's huge collection is also at Stockholm. It contains a large portion of the drawings sold at the death of Claude III Audran; in addition to works by this wonderful ornamentalist, the collection includes other important drawings and plans, possibly collected and kept in the family by earlier members of this French artistic dynasty, and many sheets pilfered by Cronstedt from the Tessin collection. The French part of the Cronstedt collection is only partly studied, photographed and published.

A catalogue of about 170 of the Stockholm drawings for and after Versailles, *Versailles à Stockholm*, was prepared for the exhibition at the Centre Culturel Suédois in Paris, September 1985.

A few other collections, such as the Berlin Kunstbibliothek and the libraries of the École des Beaux Arts and the Musée des Arts Décoratifs in Paris, have certain important sheets, but for the most part the surviving material is concentrated in the great collections mentioned above.

The early prints of Versailles are widely available in print rooms by means of the nineteenth-century republications of the Calcographie du Louvre. Almost every important engraving of Versailles is to be found in one part or another of the collections of the Cabinet des Estampes of the Paris Bibliothèque Nationale.

For painted views of Versailles the principal repository is the museum of the château itself, especially the galleries of seventeenth-century painting. Of equal interest, particularly for the fountains and gardens, is the collection of the Grand Trianon.

BIBLIOGRAPHICAL
NOTES TO THE CHAPTERS

PREFACE

ON LOUIS XIV: William F. Church, *Louis XIV in Historical Thought* (New York, 1976), provides an overview of the evolution of opinion on the personality and reign of Louis XIV. This is a long essay on historiography and has little to do with the arts. Philippe Erlanger's *Louis XIV* (English edition London and New York, 1970) is a serious modern biography, mostly developed along traditional lines but laced with facts and anecdotes provided by the *mémoire* writers of Louis's time. Nancy Mitford's *The Sun King* (London, 1966) covers in a lively manner much of the same ground more briefly, but she concentrates largely on the personal history of the king and the members of his court and their life-style. In a longish study, *Louis XIV* (New York, 1968), John Wolf gives a good narrative account of Louis's life in a traditional vein but offering an interesting, sympathetic evaluation of certain aspects of the reign often harshly judged elsewhere. Pierre Goubert, *Louis XIV and Twenty Million Frenchmen* (London and New York, 1970), looks critically at Louis's reign in terms of its impact on France at the time, but is of fundamental importance in suggesting that serious economic and social problems were more pervasive throughout the period than was heretofore believed. Excerpts from the memoirs of the Duke de Saint-Simon, *Versailles, the Court and Louis XIV*, edited by Lucy Norton (London, 1958), vividly portray the king and the world of Versailles in the words of an angry, articulate member of the court during Louis's old age.

ON LOUIS XIV AND THE ARTS: Bernard Teyssèdre's *L'Art au siècle de Louis XIV* (Paris, 1967, Livre de Poche paperback) is somewhat misnamed, since for the most part it covers far less than a century, concentrating on the years 1660–85. Though it has a somewhat overworked Marxist bias, it is far and away the most interesting book on the subject of the relationship between the art and the politics of the reign, full of interesting ideas and insights.

CHAPTER 1:
THE PERSIAN EMBASSY EXTRAORDINARY

Three principal eye-witness accounts exist of THE FIRST VISIT OF THE AMBASSADOR TO VERSAILLES. Philippe, Marquis of Dangeau, recorded it in his *Journal* (Paris, 1850) under the date of 19 February 1715, as the Duke de Saint-Simon did in his entry for the same date (*Mémoires*, ed. Borslisle, 43 vols., Paris, 1879–1928). A. and J. Marie, *Versailles au temps de Louis XIV* (Paris, 1976), reproduces the account of M. Desgranges. Both Dangeau and Saint-Simon give accounts of the final visit to Versailles in their entries for 13 August 1715. For a modern study, see Blandine Bouret, 'L'Ambassade Persane à Paris en 1715 et son image', *Gazette des Beaux Arts*, October 1982. FOR LOUIS'S GUIDE TO THE GARDENS: S. Hoog (ed.), *Manière de montrer les jardins de Versailles* (Paris, 1982).

CHAPTER 2:
THE KING, HIS ARCHITECTS AND ADMINISTRATORS

ON COLBERT: The superintendent reveals his approach in surviving documents printed in Pierre Clément (ed.), *Lettres, Instructions et Mémoires de Colbert*, Vol. V (Paris, 1868). ON MANSART: Fiske Kimball's *The Creation of the Rococo* (Philadelphia, 1943) contains in its opening 'background' chapters the only extensive discussion of Mansart's working method. ON LOUIS XIV'S MANNER OF WORKING: see John Wolf, *Louis XIV* (New York, 1968), especially Ch. XIII, 'The *Métier* of the King'.

CHAPTER 3:
THE TASTE OF THE OCCUPANTS

LOUIS XIV: The Duke de Saint-Simon paused in his *Mémoires* (op. cit.) around the time of Louis's death in 1715 to reflect on his character, the court and the royal life-style. Lucy Norton, translator and editor of Saint-Simon in *Versailles, the Court and Louis XIV* (op. cit.), gives an excellent selection of this material (from which most of the quotations used in Chapter 3 are drawn), while a more extensive presentation can be found in her three-volume edition and translation of the *Mémoires* (London, 1978).

THE DAILY ROUTINE OF LOUIS XIV: Various accounts of the daily ritual of Louis's life exist, though very little is authoritative until the famous entry in Dangeau's journal marked 'fin de l'année 1684' (Vol. 1, Paris, 1854,

87–9); an additional note at the beginning of 1686 gives the schedule of the various royal councils (p. 273). Modifications of the routine during the rest of the reign are recorded as they occur, as are all events which fall outside of the routine. A popular account, 'The King's Day', is Ch. III of Jacques Levron's *Daily Life at Versailles in the Seventeenth and Eighteenth Centuries* (London, 1968).

ON THE RELATIONSHIP OF COURT RITUAL TO THE PLAN OF ROYAL APARTMENTS: H. M. Baillie, 'Etiquette and the Planning of State Apartments in Baroque Palaces', *Archeologia*, CI. WREN ON THE TASTE OF LOUIS XIV: Quotations in Christopher Wren II, *Life and Works of Sir Christopher Wren from the 'Parentalia' or Memoires by his son, Christopher*, edited by E. J. Enthouen (London, 1903). ON CLAGNY: A. and J. Marie, *Mansart à Versailles* (2 vols., Paris, 1972), Ch. 1, provide the essential account and documentation for the history of the château. ON THE EMBROIDERY FOR THE VERSAILLES THRONE ROOM: R. A. Weigert, *Le meuble brodé de la Salle de Trône de Louis XIV* (Revue de l'art ancien et modern, 1922). ON SAINT CLOUD: The Sieur Combes (pseudonym), *Explication Historique de ce qu'il y a de plus remarquable dans la Maison Royale de Versailles et dans celle de Monsieur à S. Cloud* (Paris, 1681; English version, London, 1684), fully describes Mignard's ceiling. ON THE DUKE OF MAINE: W. H. Lewis, *The Sunset of the Splendid Century* (London, 1955), is a modern biography. ON THE DUCHESS OF BURGUNDY: In *The First Lady of Versailles* (London and Philadelphia, 1970) Lucy Norton has provided a biography largely based on Saint-Simon. ON MADAME DE MAINTENON: F. Chandernagor, *The King's Way* (New York, 1984), fiction based on her letters.

CHAPTER 4:
MONEY

ON TAXES: Ch. III of W. II. Lewis, *The Splendid Century* (Oxford, 1952), includes a brief description of the tax system. A similar and perhaps more authoritative treatment of the subject is in Ch. 3, 'Society', of Pierre Goubert's *Louis XIV and Twenty Million Frenchmen* (op. cit.). THE MARINIER CHART: Pierre Clément (ed.), *Lettres, Instructions et Mémoires de Colbert*, Vol. V (op. cit.), published the figures shown in my Table 1 as an appendix, along with another interesting table which gives a breakdown of all expenses from 1664 to 1690 by type (e.g. '*marbrerie et achates de marbre*', '*peintures et dorures, sans ... tableaux*'). ON THE FINANCIAL EFFECTS OF THE DUTCH WAR: Goubert, op. cit., Ch. VII, 'The First Turning Point'. COLBERT ON LOUIS'S BUILDINGS: Clément, op. cit., Vol.

V. ON LOUIS'S IDEAS ON BUILDING AND HIS REPUTATION: R. Guillemet, *Le Surintendance des Bâtiments du Roi, 1662–1715* (Paris, 1912), publishes Louis's admonition (recorded by Charles Perrault) to his builders on the occasion of the reorganization of the Superintendency ('I confide to you that thing which is most precious in the world to me, that is my *gloire* . . .').

CHAPTER 5:
THE ENCHANTED PALACE

ON THE FÊTE OF THE ENCHANTED ISLE: *Œuvres en vers et prose de M. de Mouighy* (Paris, 1674) reprints his account of the fête. An officially published account was in the *Gazette*, No. 60: *Les Particularités des divertissements pris à Versailles par Leurs Majestés*. In 1673 the Royal Printing Office reissued another official description with nine folio plates by Israel Silvestre; for five of these and various drawings, see A. Marie, *Naissance de Versailles*, Vol. I (Paris, 1968). SAINT-SIMON ON VERSAILLES: In the *Mémoires* for 1715. ON THE FIRST CHÂTEAU: P. de Nolhac, *La Création de Versailles* (Paris, 1901), Ch. 1, and Marie, *Naissance* (op. cit.). ON THE GARDEN: P. Verlet, *Versailles* (Paris, 1961); G. Weber, 'Die Versailles-Konzepte von André Le Nôtre', *Münchner Jahrbuch der Bildenden Kunst*, Rd. 20, 1969; W. H. Adams, *The French Garden, 1500–1800* (New York, 1979). ON COLBERT'S LETTER: Clément, op. cit., Vol. V. ON BERNINI'S VISIT TO VERSAILLES: P. F. de Chantelou, *Journal du Voyage en France du Cavalier Bernin* (Paris, 1885), entry for 13 September 1665. ON THE GALLERY OF BEAUTIES: Exhibition Catalogue, *Les salons littéraires au XVII siècle* (Bibliothèque Nationale, p. XII, Paris, 1968). ON THE GROTTO OF THETIS PROGRAMME: Madeleine de Scúdéry, *La promenade de Versailles, dédiée au Roi* (Paris, 1669). ON THE LATONA THEME: Nathan T. Whitman, 'Myth and Politics: Versailles and the Fountain of Latona', *Louis XIV and the Craft of Kingship*, ed. Rule (Columbus, Ohio, 1969). ON THE EARLY PALACE PROJECT: Jean Claude Le Guillou, 'Aperçu sur un projet insolite (1668) pour le château de Versailles', *Gazette des Beaux Arts*, February 1980.

CHAPTER 6:
THE ENVELOPPE

ON THE VARIOUS PROJECTS FOR A NEW PALACE AND THE CRISIS: R. Berger, 'The Chronology of the Enveloppe of Versailles', *Architectura*, Vol. 10, 1980. COLBERT'S MEMOS ON SEVERAL PROJECTS FOR VERSAILLES: Clément, op. cit., Vol. V. ON THE LE VAU PROJECT IN STOCK-

HOLM: A. Marie, *Naissance de Versailles* (op. cit.), Vol. I, discussed the design extensively after its initial publication with little commentary by Fiske Kimball in the *Gazette des Beaux Arts*, 1948. Marie's dating of the Le Vau project to 1665 has not been accepted by subsequent writers. ON THE COLONNA ROOMS: Antoine Schnapper, 'Colonna, etc. ...', *Bulletin de la Société de l'histoire de l'art français* (Année 1966). ON THE ORGANIZATION OF THE ROYAL APARTMENTS IN THE PALACE OF 1669: H. M. Baillie, 'Etiquette and the Planning of State Apartments in Baroque Palaces', *Archeologia*, CI.

CHAPTER 7:
THE PALACE OF APOLLO

FÉLIBIEN'S GUIDE: André Félibien, *Description sommaire du château de Versailles* (Paris, 1674). ON THE MEANING OF MYTHOLOGICAL SUBJECTS IN THE PAINTING OF THE TIME OF LOUIS XIV: Jennifer Montagu, 'On the Painted Enigma in French Seventeenth-century Art', *Journal of the Warburg and Courtauld Institutes*, XXXI, 1968. ON THE SCULPTURES ON THE FAÇADE OF THE PALACE: François Souchal, 'Les Statues aux façades du Château de Versailles', *Gazette des Beaux Arts*, February 1972. ON THE MARSY BROTHERS' WORKS ON THE FAÇADES OF VERSAILLES: Thomas Hedin, *The Sculpture of Gaspard and Balthazard Marsy* (Columbia, Missouri, 1983). ON THE PROGRAMME OF THE GRAND COMMAND: Claude Nivelon, *Vie de Charles Le Brun* (MS., Bibliothèque Nationale, MS. fr. 12987); excerpt in Nolhac, *La Création de Versailles* (op. cit.). ON THE DECOR OF THE GRAND APARTMENTS: Antoine Schnapper, *Jean Jouvenet: Les débuts de la grande decoration* (Paris, 1974), gives an excellent résumé of the limits of our knowledge of the history of these decorations. Malcolm Campbell, *Pietro da Cortona at the Pitti Palace* (Princeton, 1977), gives a full account of the Pitti decor and contrasts it with that of Versailles ('The Planetary Rooms and the Seventeenth Century'). ON THE LOUVRE DECOR: André Félibien, *Entretiens sur les vies et les ouvrages des plus excellents peintres ...* (Paris, 1688). COMBES' GUIDE: The Sieur Combes, *Explication Historique de ce qu'il y a de plus remarquable dans la Maison Royale de Versailles ...* (op. cit.). ON LE BRUN AND THE FOUNTAINS: Gerold Weber, *French Fountains during the Reign of Louis XIV* (1985). ON GENERAL ISSUES OF THE ICONOGRAPHY OF THE SUN, the pre-history of Louis's symbol: Ernst Kantorowicz in *Dumbarton Oaks Papers*, No. 17, Cambridge, Mass., 1963. Louis Hautecœur, *Louis XIV, Roi-Soleil* (Paris, 1953).

CHAPTER 8:
NEW ATTITUDES

COLBERT ON ROYAL BUILDING: Clément, op. cit., Vol. V. ON THE
MEETING OF THE COUNCIL ON THE HALL OF MIRRORS: Nivelon,
op. cit. ON LOUIS'S EXPLOITS IN TAPESTRY: Daniel Meyer, *L'Histoire
du Roy* (Paris, 1980), gives an extended account of the weaving of the
tapestries and a description and explanation of the fourteen completed
tapestries of the second series. ON THE INTERPRETATION OF THE SUB-
JECTS OF THE HALL OF MIRRORS: W. Vitzthum and S. Hoog, *Charles
LeBrun à Versailles: la Galerie des Glaces* (Paris, 1969). A SEVENTEENTH-
CENTURY DESCRIPTION OF THE HALL OF MIRRORS: François Blon-
del, *Cours professés à l'Académie d'Architecture, 1675-1685* (second ed. Paris,
1698). ON MANSART'S WORKING METHOD: Fiske Kimball, *The Creation
of the Rococo* (op. cit.).

CHAPTER 9:
JOURS D'APPARTEMENT

BOURDELOT'S DESCRIPTION: Pierre de Nolhac, *Versailles Résidence de
Louis XIV* (Paris, 1925), prints an extended extract from the book.
SCUDÉRY'S DESCRIPTION: Extensively quoted in Nolhac, op. cit. THE
MERCURE GALANT DESCRIPTION: Also in Nolhac, op. cit. ON INTER-
IOR DECORATION IN SEVENTEENTH-CENTURY FRANCE: Peter
Thornton, *Seventeenth-Century Interior Decoration in England, France and
Holland* (New Haven, 1978). ON THE SILVERSMITH BALLIN: Hugh
Honour, *Goldsmiths and Silversmiths* (New York, 1971), and Y. Bottineau
and O. Lefuel, *Les Grands Orfèvres* (Paris, 1965). Ballin is mostly given
credit for the design of the Versailles silver furniture. He died in 1678, years
before work began on 'the appartment'. THE FUNDAMENTAL SOURCE
FOR THE FURNISHINGS OF VERSAILLES: J. Guiffrey (ed.), *Inventaires
... 1663 à 1715* (Paris, 1885).

CHAPTER 10:
COLBERT AND LOUVOIS

BIOGRAPHY OF LOUVOIS: Camille Rousset, *Histoire de Louvois* ... (4
vols., Paris, 1879), brings together the documentation and provides the basic

account of the life of the minister. BIOGRAPHY OF COLBERT AND ACCOUNTS OF HIS LAST DAYS: Pierre Clément, *Histoire de Colbert ...* (2 vols., Paris, 1874). ON THE GRAND COMMUN: A. and J. Marie, *Mansart à Versailles*, Vol. I (Paris, 1972), publish the basic information. ON THE DRAWINGS BY CRUYL: G. Walton, 'Liévin Cruyl's Drawings for Versailles', *Essays in Honor of H. W. Janson* (New York, 1981). ON THE STABLES: A. and J. Marie, *Mansart à Versailles*, Vol. I (op. cit.), gives the plans, payments etc. ON THE REBUILDING OF THE COUR DE MARBRE: Jean Claude Le Guillou, 'Remarques sur le Corps Central du Château de Versailles', *Gazette des Beaux Arts*, February 1976. LOUVOIS'S CORRESPONDENCE WITH PUGET: L. Lagrange, *Pierre Puget* (Marseilles, 1868). The standard monograph on Puget is by Klaus Herding, *Pierre Puget ...* (Berlin, 1970). ON LE BRUN'S FALL: Catalogue of the exhibition *Charles Le Brun* (Versailles, 1963). ON THE ORANGERY AND THE SUMS SPENT ON IT: A. and J. Marie, *Mansart à Versailles*, Vol. II (op. cit.). LE NÔTRE ON THE COLONNADE: The remark is included in the memoirs of Saint-Simon written on the occasion of Le Nôtre's death in 1700. ON THE SCULPTURAL PROGRAMME OF THE COLONNADE: P. de Nolhac, 'L'achèvement des jardins', *Versailles Résidence de Louis XIV* (op. cit.). ON THE 'SUJETS DE LA FABLE': Edith Standen, 'The *Sujets de la Fable ...* Gobelins Tapestries', *Art Bulletin*, June 1964, has given most of the interesting details of the changes at the Gobelins after Le Brun's removal. ON THE PROJECTS FOR THE NEW CHAPEL AND THEIR RELATIONSHIP TO THE PLANNING OF THE INVALIDES: Patrik Reutersvärd, *The Two Churches of the Hôtel des Invalides* (Stockholm, 1965).

CHAPTER 11:
GRAND TRIANON

FOR THE HISTORY OF THE CONSTRUCTION OF THE GRAND TRIANON AND IMPORTANT DOCUMENTATION: Bertrand Jestaz, 'Le Trianon de marbre ou Louis XIV architecte', *Gazette des Beaux Arts*, November 1969. A DOCUMENTARY HISTORY OF GRAND TRIANON, FEATURING THE PAINTINGS COMMISSIONED FOR IT: Antoine Schnapper, *Tableaux pour le Trianon de marbre, 1688-1714* (Paris, 1967). FOR LE NÔTRE'S DESCRIPTION: Ragnar Josephson, 'Le Grand Trianon sous Louis XIV', *Revue de l'histoire de Versailles et de Seine-et-Oise*, 1927.

CHAPTER 12:
TECHNOLOGY

ON OBTAINING WATER FOR VERSAILLES: P. de Nolhac, 'Le Grand
Parc et les eaux', *Versailles Résidence de Louis XIV* (op. cit.), gives a full
and clear description with quotations from some sources. ON THE INTER-
IOR COLLAPSE OF THE WALLS: Oral communication of Daniel Meyer.
Payments for the repairs are to be found in the Maison du Roi documents
of the eighteenth century. ON THE SEIGNELAY HARDWARE: ed. Weigert
etc., *Relations Artistiques entre la France et la Suède* ... (1692; Stockholm,
1964). FOR THE FIGURES OF THE VARIOUS EXPENSES FOR VER-
SAILLES, INCLUDING THE OBTAINING OF WATER: Chart of expenses
by Marinier (1691), published as an appendix in P. Clément (ed.), *Lettres
... de Colbert*, Vol. V (op. cit.); Table 1, p. 50, here. PERRAULT ME-
MOIRS: Charles Perrault, *Mémoires de ma vie* (ed. Bonnelon, Paris, 1909).
SCULPTURES OF THE PARK: S. Thomassin, *Recueil des figures* ... (Paris,
1694).

CHAPTER 13:
VERSAILLES IN AN ERA OF POLITICAL AND
MILITARY DISASTER

ON THE POLITICAL AND MILITARY SITUATION OF THE 1680S: See the
biographies of Louis XIV by Wolf, Erlanger and Goubert mentioned above
in the Bibliographical Notes to the Preface. FOR THE SOURCHES QUO-
TATIONS: Marquis de Sourches, *Mémoires: Secrets et Inédits de la Cour de
France*, Vol. III (Paris, 1682-93); excerpts in A. and J. Marie, *Mansart à
Versailles*, Vol. II (op. cit.). FÉLIBIEN'S GUIDE: André Félibien des Avaux,
Description de Versailles, ancienne et nouvelle (Paris, 1703). PIGANOL'S
GUIDE: Piganol de la Force, *Nouvelle description des châteaux et parcs de
Versailles* (Paris, 1701). ON THE PAINTINGS FOR THE OVAL SALON
ETC.: Antoine Schnapper, 'Two Unknown Ceiling Paintings by Mignard for
Louis XIV', *Art Bulletin*, March 1974. LOUIS'S COMMENTS ON THE
DECOR OF THE ZOO: Document at the Musée du Château, Versailles. ON
THE INTERIORS OF THE ZOO: F. Kimball, *The Creation of the Rococo*
(op. cit.).

CHAPTER 14:
THE LAST GREAT WORKS

CRONSTRÖM'S REMARKS: ed. Weigert etc., *Relations Artistiques entre la France et la Suède ...* (Stockholm, 1964). DANGEAU'S JOURNAL: op. cit. (see under Ch. 1 above). HARDOUIN-MANSART'S PAPERS: Unpublished. Archives Nationales, o¹1473 and o¹1809. ON THE SCULPTURES FOR MARLY: Betsy Rosasco, 'New Documents and Drawings Concerning Lost Statues from the Château of Marly', *Metropolitan Museum Journal* Vol. 10, 1975, and her unpublished dissertation, *The Sculptures of Marly* (New York University, 1980). ON THE HISTORY OF THE CHAPEL (including expenditures): A. and J. Marie, *Versailles au temps de Louis XIV* (op. cit.). ON THE PROGRAMME OF THE CHAPEL: Pierre de Nolhac, *La Chapelle Royale de Versailles* (Paris, 1913). ON MARLY: Gerold Weber, *Wienes Jahrbuch* XXVIII, 1975.

CHAPTER 15:
CONCLUSION

ON TESSIN'S PROJECTS: ed. Weigert etc., *Relations Artistiques entre la France et la Suède ...*, 1714, 1715 (op. cit.). ON DANIEL MAROT: F. Kimball, 'Background', *The Creation of the Rococo* (op. cit.). ON THE BUILDING OF BLENHEIM: Geoffrey Webb (ed.), *The Complete Works of John Vanbrugh*, Vol. IV (London, 1928), and Kerry Downes, *Hawksmoor* (London, 1969).

NOTES
ON THE TEXT

1. B. Jestaz, 'Le Trianon de marbre ou Louis XIV architecte', *Gazette des Beaux Arts*, November 1969.

2. H. M. Baillie, 'Etiquette and the Planning of State Apartments in Baroque Palaces', *Archeologia*, CI, describes divergent national practices in the arrangements of apartments.

3. Christopher Wren, *Parentalia* (London, 1903).

4. P. Verlet, *Versailles* (Paris, 1961), pp. 29–38, gives the best short account of the influences on the taste of the young Louis XIV, both personal and architectural.

5. L. Norton (ed.), *Versailles, the Court and Louis XIV* (London, 1958), has provided me with the translations from Saint-Simon's memoirs which I have used throughout this book. Other translations are by myself.

6. K. O. Johnson, 'Il n'y a plus de Pyrénées', *Gazette des Beaux Arts*, January 1981, stresses this point and, in my opinion, somewhat over-argues it.

7. See R. Berger, *Antoine Le Pautre* (New York, 1969), pp. 77–83.

8. To the traditional taxes (the Faille, Gabelle and the Aides) only one was added as late as 1695, the Capitation, a poll tax.

9. See *Œuvres en vers et prose de M. de Mouighy* (Paris, 1674).

10. P. Clément (ed.), *Lettres . . . de Colbert*, Vol. V (Paris, 1868).

11. P. F. de Chantelou, *Journal du Voyage en France du Cavalier Bernin* (Paris, 1889), entry for 13 September 1665.

12. Clément, op. cit., Vol. V.

13. See note 3.

14. As noted by G. Weber in the *Münchner Jahrbuch*, 1969.

15. This point has frequently been made and is the subject of an article by N. T. Whitman in *Louis XIV and the Craft of Kingship*, ed. Rule (Columbus, Ohio, 1969).

16. J. C. Le Guillou, 'Aperçu sur un projet insolite (1668) pour le château de Versailles', *Gazette des Beaux Arts*, February 1980.

17. R. Berger, 'The Chronology of the Enveloppe of Versailles', *Architectura*, Vol. 10, 1980, has at last made the major step in determining this difficult chronology. His article corrects my own in *BSHAF*, 1976, and I have adopted his arguments here.

18. Clément, op. cit., Vol. V, p. 284.

19. Baillie, op. cit., gives the best description of baroque state apartments.

20. M. Campbell, *Pietro da Cortona at the Pitti Palace* (Princeton, 1977), has discussed the programme, and some of his descriptions are used in my text.

21. A. Félibien, *Entretiens sur les vies et les ouvrages des plus excellents peintres* ... (Paris, 1688).

22. These questions are raised by Jennifer Montagu, 'On the Painted Enigma in French Seventeenth-century Art', *Journal of the Warburg and Courtauld Institutes*, XXXI, 1968.

23. Cabinet des Dessins, Louvre, No. 5737-29639. The drawing shows an end of the gallery with Apollo and Diana above the architrave. The door opening shows alternative projects: wood panelling and panes of glass. Since the door leads to a neighbouring room the glass must be mirrored, thus dating that aspect of the decor from the time of Le Brun's first project.

24. Two distinct projects for the historical theme project are known: the one as executed and another shown in a drawing at the Cabinet des Dessins, Louvre, No. 5801-27702.

25. This point was made in W. Vitzthum and S. Hoog, *Charles LeBrun à Versailles: la Galerie des Glaces* (Paris, 1969).

26. Vitzthum, op. cit.

27. J. F. Blondel, *L'Architecture française* (Paris, 1698, second edition).

28. Bourdelot *père*, *Relation des assemblées faites à Versailles* ... (Paris, 1683).

29. Hugh Honour, *Cabinet Makers and Furniture Designers* (London, 1969).

30. L. Lagrange, *Pierre Puget* (Paris, 1868), p. 191. The Louvois-Puget correspondence is to be found in the following chapter.

31. For an example of Mansart's power, note the story of Puget's Place Royale in Marseilles; see Lagrange, op. cit.

32. See F. Hamilton Hazlehurst, *Gardens of Illusion ... Le Nostre* (Nashville, 1980), p. 126.

33. There is some controversy about a point made by P. de Nolhac, *Versailles Résidence de Louis XIV* (Paris, 1925). Robert Berger suggests (orally) that the sculpture subjects Nolhac mentions may only refer to reliefs.

34. P. Reutersvärd, *The Two Churches of the Hôtel des Invalides* (Stockholm, 1965).

35. This quotation is from B. Jestaz, 'Le Trianon de marbre ou Louis XIV architecte', *Gazette des Beaux Arts*, November 1969. Jestaz also published the Louvois–Mansart correspondence concerning Trianon. The Tessin quotation may be found there as well.

36. F. Kimball, *The Creation of the Rococo* (Philadelphia, 1943).

37. C. Tadgell, *Ange-Jacques Gabriel* (London, 1978), p. 32.

38. P. de Nolhac, *Versailles Résidence de Louis XIV* (Paris, 1925), made this important observation. Much of my account of the attempt to find water for Versailles is taken directly from this book.

39. P. Goubert, *Louis XIV and Twenty Million Frenchmen* (London and New

York, 1970). Goubert gives a compelling account of the financial problems resulting from the Dutch War.

40. J. Wolf, *Louis XIV* (New York, 1968), p. 446.

41. This observation was made after careful study of the inventories of Versailles by Sir Francis Watson, who presented this material at the Metropolitan Museum (Wrightsman Lectures, 1981).

42. A. and J. Marie, *Mansart à Versailles*, Vol. II (Paris, 1972), pp. 501–3.

43. F. Kimball, op. cit., p. 49.

44. A. Schnapper, 'Two Unknown Ceiling Paintings by Mignard for Louis XIV', *Art Bulletin*, March 1974.

45. This document is in the collection of the Musée du Château, Versailles.

46. Kimball, op. cit., p. 56.

47. Bérain was a somewhat embattled figure. Audran successfully imitated aspects of his style and became the dauphin's principal decorator at Meudon (see Kimball, op. cit., p. 62).

48. Two important river groups now decorate the west basin area of the Tuileries gardens in Paris.

49. Kimball, op. cit., p. 67.

50. A. Schnapper, *Tableaux pour le Trianon de marbre 1688–1714* (Paris, 1967).

51. P. de Nolhac, *La Chapelle Royale de Versailles* (Paris, 1913), reproduces the description of the programme by Félibien the younger, who may have been the author of it. Félibien gives very limited indications of its meaning. My understanding is that there are several important messages: (1) the rich variety of themes covering many aspects of Christian belief is unique in its time and comparable only to the programmes of the great medieval cathedrals; this is then a neo-medieval church; (2) the continuity of the religious traditions of France from Charlemagne to Saint Louis and beyond is stressed; (3) the shape of the building and references to many of Saint Louis's collections of relics suggest an attempt to create a new Sainte Chapelle; (4) the theme of the building of a new Jerusalem also appears in the chapel decor and inscriptions.

52. Kimball, op. cit., p. 83.

LIST OF
ILLUSTRATIONS

Mirrors on 19 February 1715 (M.V. 5641). Painting. Versailles, Musée du Château. Photo: Bulloz.

13. Anonymous: *déjeuner* of the Persian ambassador at Versailles. Pencil and ink drawing. Versailles, Musée Lambinet. Photo: Bulloz.

14. The Queen's Stairway. Versailles. Photo: Réunion des Musées Nationaux.

15. New plan of the town, château and gardens of Versailles, 1719. Engraving. Paris, Bibliothèque Nationale. Photo: Bibliothèque Nationale.

16. J.B. Martin: bird's-eye view of the north axis of the park of Versailles seen from above the Basin of Neptune (M.V. 751). Painting, *c.* 1700. Versailles, Grand Trianon. Photo: Réunion des Musées Nationaux.

17. *Le Théâtre d'eau*, the water theatre *bosquet*. Drawing. Paris, Bibliothèque Nationale. Photo: Bibliothèque Nationale.

18. Israel Silvestre: view of the Bosquet of the Three Fountains in the garden of Versailles. Engraving, 1684. Paris, Bibliothèque Nationale. Photo: Bibliothèque Nationale.

19. P. Brissard: perspectival view of the château of Vincennes on the side with the entry to the park (south). Engraving. Paris, Bibliothèque Nationale. Photo: Bibliothèque Nationale.

20. Louis Le Vau and André Le Nôtre: château of Vaux-le-Vicomte, 1657–61. Photo: Aerofilms.

21. *Meuble brodé dans la Salle d'Audience de l'Appartement à Versailles* (T.H.C. 1554). Coloured drawing. Stockholm, Nationalmuseum. Photo: Nationalmuseum.

22*a*. Israel Silvestre: view of the royal château of Versailles. Engraving from the series *Maisons Royales*, 1652. Paris, Bibliothèque Nationale. Photo: Bibliothèque Nationale.

22*b*. Plan of the ground floor of the château of Versailles. Drawing, before 1662. Paris, Bibliothèque Nationale. Photo: Bibliothèque Nationale.

23. Adam-François Van der Meulen: view of the château and Orangery of Versailles seen from the south (Satory hill) (M.V. 725). Painting, 1664. Versailles, Musée du Château. Photo: Réunion des Musées Nationaux.

24. Aveline: view of the salon and grotto of the zoo (Ménagerie) and some of the cages. Versailles, Musée du Château. Photo: Réunion des Musées Nationaux.

25. *Plan original du Chasteau et Petit Parc de Versailles comme il esté Encienne-ment avant que le Roy y est fait travailler*. Coloured drawing, *c.* 1664. Paris, Bibliothèque de l'Institut. Photo: Giraudon.

26. Plan of the Versailles park showing the ground plans of the structures built for the *fête* of 1668. Coloured drawing. Paris, Bibliothèque Nationale. Photo: Bibliothèque Nationale.

27. Perelle: the Grotto of Thetis. Engraving, before 1670. Paris, Bibliothèque Nationale. Photo: Bibliothèque Nationale.

28. Jean-Baptist Tuby: Apollo rising from the sea. Versailles, the Basin of Apollo. Photo: Giraudon.

29. Pierre Le Pautre: the Fountain of Latona. Engraving after the sculptures of the Marsy brothers, 1678. Paris, Bibliothèque Nationale. Photo: Bibliothèque Nationale.

now in an eighteenth-century setting designed by Hubert Robert. Marble sculpture, 1666–72. Versailles, Gardens. Photo: Réunion des Musées Nationaux.

46. The Fountain of the Crane and the Swan in the labyrinth of Versailles. Engraving by Le Clerc. Paris, Bibliothèque Nationale. Photo: Bibliothèque Nationale.

47. Balthazard and Gaspard Marsy: female figures representing January and February, on the central portion of the garden façade of the château. Stone sculptures, 1670–72. Versailles. Photo: Hedin.

48. Attributed to the Marsy brothers: keystone of the eighteenth arch of the ground floor of the garden façade, in the form of an old woman's head. Stone sculpture, 1673 or 1674. Versailles. Photo: Hedin.

49. Plan of the château, gardens and town of Versailles, detail (Inv. 33014). Drawing, inscribed '1680'. Paris, Louvre, Cabinet des Dessins. Photo: Réunion des Musées Nationaux.

50. Project for a western parterre in front of the garden façade of Versailles, shown as it would have been seen from the terrace (G.M. 8171). Drawing, c. 1673–4. Paris, Louvre, Cabinet des Dessins. Photo: Réunion des Musées Nationaux.

51. Charles Le Brun: the Four Seasons, a project for four statues of the Grand Command (G.M. 5956). Drawing, c. 1674. Paris, Louvre, Cabinet des Dessins. Photo: Réunion des Musées Nationaux.

52. René Houasse and others: *Venus Crowned* and other scenes of the loves of princes and mythological scenes. Painted ceiling, before 1681. Versailles, Salon of Venus. Photo: Réunion des Musées Nationaux.

53. Charles de Lafosse and others: *Apollo in his Chariot* and other historical and mythological scenes. Painted ceiling, 1670s. Versailles, Salon of Apollo. Photo: Réunion des Musées Nationaux.

54. Israel Silvestre: the Fountain of Fame at Versailles (a *bosquet*). Engraving, 1682. Collection of the author. Photo: Fink.

55. Workshop of Mansart: elevation with cross-sections, seen from the east, of a project for the vertical expansion of the palace of Versailles, detail. Coloured drawing, probably 1678. Paris, Archives Nationales. Photo: Archives Nationales.

56. Workshop of Mansart: southern elevation showing the vertical expansion of the northern part of the château of Versailles (with a cross-section of the proposed interior of the central *corps de logis*, including a great gallery and a high salon). Coloured drawing, probably 1678. Paris, Archives Nationales. Photo: Archives Photographiques.

57. Workshop of Mansart: southern elevation of the northern part of the château of Versailles as it stood about 1678, with cross-sections showing the interiors of a great gallery and salon. Coloured drawing, probably 1678. Paris, Archives Nationales. Photo: Archives Photographiques.

58. Workshop of Mansart: elevation of the north walls of the new gallery and salon of the château of Versailles. Drawing, inscribed as approved for execution, dated 26 September 1678 and signed 'Colbert' (G.M. 8438). Paris, Louvre, Cabinet des Dessins. Photo: Réunion des Musées Nationaux.

59. Capital of a pilaster using Mansart's 'French order'. Versailles, Hall of Mirrors. Photo: Archives Photographiques.

76. Baudoin Yvart: a brasero or incense burner on its stand (M.V. 7057). Study for a Gobelins tapestry of the series *Les Maisons du Roi*. Painting, *c.* 1673. Versailles, Musée du Château. Photo: Réunion des Musées Nationaux.

77. Jean Bérain: the Hall of Mirrors furnished and with the addition of many silver pieces from the Salon of Apollo (throne room) on the occasion of the embassy from Siam. Engraving, 1686. Versailles, Musée du Château. Photo: Réunion des Musées Nationaux.

78. A chandelier representing Fame, similar to one described by Tessin as in the Grand Apartment of the King at Versailles (C.C. 1549). Drawing, probably after a Le Brun design and possibly by Claude Ballin, before 1678. Stockholm, Nationalmuseum. Photo: Nationalmuseum.

79. After Charles Le Brun: designs for large console tables; one is similar to one of the silver tables shown in an engraving of the Hall of Mirrors (C.C. 2389). Drawing. Stockholm, Nationalmuseum. Photo: Nationalmuseum.

80. Daniel Marot: furniture for an area between two windows of a room at Het Loo, Apeldoorn. Drawing, dated 1701. Amsterdam, Rijksmuseum. Photo: Rijksmuseum.

81. Gian Lorenzo Bernini: bust of Louis XIV. Marble sculpture, 1665. Versailles, Salon of Diana (see Fig. 9). Photo: Giraudon.

82. Attributed to Domenico Cucci: a large wall cabinet, said to have been made for the Small Apartment of the King at Versailles. Ebony, gilded metal and wood, with stone and intarsia decorations, 1681–3. Alnwick Castle, collection of the Duke of Northumberland. Photo: English Life Publications Ltd.

83. After Charles Le Brun: *Louis XIV's Visit to the Gobelins*. Tapestry, *c.* 1729, the sixth series. Paris, Mobilier National. Photo: Bulloz.

84. Anonymous: solid silver furniture in a throne room (at Versailles?). Drawing *c.* 1683. Berlin: Kunstbibliothek. Photo: Staatliche Museen Preussischer Kulturbesitz, Berlin (West).

85. Anonymous: Madame de Montespan reclining on a day bed above a gallery at Clagny. Painting, 1670s? Florence, Uffizi Gallery. Photo: Alinari.

86. Workshop of Mansart: elevation of one side of the Grand Commun of Versailles (T.H.C. 2423). Drawing, *c.* 1679. Stockholm, Nationalmuseum. Photo: Nationalmuseum.

87. Liévin Cruyl: bird's-eye view of Versailles from the east, with various projects added. Drawing, 1683/4. Versailles, Musée du Château. Photo: Réunion des Musées Nationaux.

88. Jean-Baptiste Martin: view from the Cour de Marbre of the château of Versailles, across the Cour d'Armes to the Grande and Petite Écuries (stables), with the Avenue de Paris in the background (M.V. 748). Painting, after 1700. Versailles, Musée du Château. Photo: Réunion des Musées Nationaux.

89. Israel Silvestre: bird's-eye view of Versailles seen from the direction of the Satory hill (south) (Inv. 33055). Drawing, 1683–91. Paris, Louvre, Cabinet des Dessins. Photo: Réunion des Musées Nationaux.

90. Liévin Cruyl: bird's-eye view of the palace of Versailles seen from the west. Drawing, dated 1684. Versailles, Musée du Château. Photo: Réunion des Musées Nationaux.

109. Plan of the Grand Trianon with the central pavilion of the Trianon de Porcelaine preserved (Cabinet des Estampes Va. 448 f). Drawing (now lost), 1687. Paris, Bibliothèque Nationale. Photo from Marie, *Versailles au Temps de Louis XIV*.

110. Pierre Denis Martin: the Grand Trianon as built (M.V. 760). Painting, after 1700. Versailles, Musée du Château. Photo: Réunion des Musées Nationaux.

111. Elevation of a large vestibule for the château of Versailles, a rejected project which appears on the same sheet as our Fig. 42. Coloured drawing, 1670s. Paris, École des Beaux Arts. Photo: Giraudon.

112. The gallery of the Grand Trianon. *c.* 1687. Photo: Réunion des Musées Nationaux.

113. Ground plan of one project for the King's Bathroom at Versailles (C.C. 397). Coloured drawing, *c.* 1671. Stockholm, Nationalmuseum. Photo: Nationalmuseum.

114. Charles Le Brun: tritons and nereids, project of a relief decoration for the King's Bathroom at Versailles (G.M. 8226). Paris, Louvre, Cabinet des Dessins. Photo: Réunion des Musées Nationaux.

115. Elevation of the great aqueduct of Maintenon, detail (C.C. 655). Drawing, *c.* 1684. Stockholm, Nationalmuseum. Photo: Nationalmuseum.

116. The Marly Machine. Engraving, *c.* 1686. Paris, Bibliothèque Nationale. Photo: Bibliothèque Nationale.

117. The *parterre d'eau*, Versailles. Photograph by Eugène Atget, July 1901. New York, Museum of Modern Art, Abbott-Levy Collection. Photo: Museum of Modern Art.

118. Antoine Coysevox: *The Garonne*, a river god. Sculpture, dated 1686, cast in bronze after 1688. Versailles, *parterre d'eau*. Photo: Bulloz.

119. Antoine Coysevox: the Vase of War (illustrating the war against the Turks in Hungary). Marble sculpture, 1684. Versailles, corner of the palace terrace. Photo: Giraudon.

120. Martin Desjardins: *Diana* (the *Evening*, from the series *The Four Times of the Day*). Marble sculpture, 1680. Versailles, by the north water *cabinet*. Photo: Bulloz.

121. The Allée Royale, looking east (with the marble statue of *Cyparisse* by A. Flamen, 1696). Versailles. Photo: Bulloz.

122. Charles-André Boulle: commode for the king's bedroom at the grand Trianon. Ebony wood with inlays of exotic woods, tortoiseshell and gilt bronze with cast bronze gilt ornaments. *c.* 1706. Versailles, Musée du Château. Photo: Giraudon.

123. Gobelins manufactory: door panel from a cabinet representing the French cock triumphant over the eagle of the Empire and the lion of Spain. Inlay of various exotic and coloured woods. 1670s. Malibu, J. Paul Getty Museum. Photo: J. Paul Getty Museum.

124. Floor plan of the Premier Étage of the old château of Versailles with the additions and changes of 1692, including the Oval Salon and next to it the Shell Room. Drawing, after 1701. Paris, Archives Nationales. Photo: Archives Photographiques.

125. A pedestal made for the Oval Salon and the bronze reduction of François Girardon's *Pluto abducting Persephone* which stood on it. Drawing. Berlin,

143. Antoine Coypel: study for an Old Testament prophet for the ceiling of the chapel of Versailles (Inv. 25825 *bis*). Drawing, *c.* 1709. Paris, Louvre, Cabinet des Dessins. Photo: Réunion des Musées Nationaux.

144. Attributed to René Charpentier: *Grace*, a trophy representing the Holy Spirit and baptism (*The Baptism of Christ?*) for the chapel of Versailles (T.H.C. 1004). Drawing, inscribed 'Charpentier', *c.* 1708. Stockholm, Nationalmuseum. Photo: Nationalmuseum.

145. Chandelier and garlands, bottom portion of a trophy decorating a pier of the ambulatory. Relief sculpture, *c.* 1708. Versailles, chapel. Photo: Réunion des Musées Nationaux.

146. View of the south aisle of the ground floor of the chapel. Versailles. Photo: Bulloz.

147. Study for a confessional for the chapel of Versailles. Drawing, *c.* 1709-10. Paris, Archives Nationales. Photo: Archives Nationales.

148. Attributed to Pierre Le Pautre: organ case. Carved wood, 1709-10. Versailles, tribune of the chapel above the altar. Photo: Bulloz.

149. Plan of the chapel, its vestibule and the new salon connecting the chapel with the Grand Apartment at Versailles. Drawing, *c.* 1711. Paris, Bibliothèque Nationale. Photo: Bibliothèque Nationale.

150. Jean Hardy: the Children's Island. Lead sculpture, 1710. Versailles, gardens. Photo: Bulloz.

151. Nicodemus Tessin the younger: exterior elevation of the pavilion of Apollo for Versailles (T.H.C. 1199). Stockholm, Nationalmuseum. Photo: Nationalmuseum.

152. J. B. Fischer von Erlach: ideal design for Schönbrunn (near Vienna). Engraving, design from *c.* 1693. Photo: Bibliothèque Nationale.

153. Lukas von Hildebrandt: the Upper Belvedere, Vienna, seen from below on the garden side. Photo: A. F. Kersting.

154. John Vanbrugh and Nicholas Hawksmoor: Blenheim Palace, Oxfordshire, the north front. 1705-16. Photo: A. F. Kersting.

ILLUSTRATION
ACKNOWLEDGEMENTS

INDEX

Note: Italicized page numbers indicate illustrations